First published in Great Britain in 2007 by Atlantic Books,
an imprint of Grove Atlantic Ltd.

This trade paperback edition published in Great Britain in 2008
by Atlantic Books.

9 8 7 6 5 4 3 2 1

A CIP catalogue record for this book is available from the
British Library.

ISBN: 978 1 84354 663 4

Produced by Essential Works
www.essentialworks.co.uk
Editor: Mal Peachey
Designer: Kate Ward

Atlantic Books
An imprint of Grove Atlantic Ltd
Ormond House
26–27 Boswell Street
London WC1N 3JZ

Printed in Singapore

THE COMPLETE AND UTTER AWFULNESS OF THE ENGLAND FOOTBALL TEAM SINCE 1966

Atlantic Books

London

CONTENTS

INTRODUCTION

'The only team we have beaten of any real substance in a major championships in the last three events is Argentina in 2002, so why do we always go into a tournament with a belief that we will win it, only to be found wanting when the competition starts to heat up at the quarter-final stage? There has to be an acceptance that the future is not bright and our ability to compete on the world stage is declining before any improvement can be undertaken.'

This quote is taken from a report commissioned by the Football Association and written by David Platt in 2003, updated for presentation to Trevor Brooking, the FA's director of football development, in 2007. It was updated to commemorate the tenth anniversary of the establishment of the FA Charter for Quality, which was supposed to nurture young English talent with a view to winning trophies. That it was the tenth anniversary of something begun by Howard Wilkinson is surprising (he is a man who has left little else to English football, after all). But what is astounding is that the FA have publicly admitted that they are not doing something correctly. Platt's report states on the original aims of the Charter: 'The boast was that, by 2006, we would have a squad which would meet every criterion for success, and winning the World Cup in Germany was the objective that was believed to be very much achievable.'

In many ways it is that belief which this book deals with. As Platt's report goes on to say, 'We are all aware of what happened in Germany 2006, when we never looked capable of winning the trophy.' He might have added, just as we're all aware of what happened in 1970, 1982, 1986, 1990, 1998 and 2002, when English fans and the FA believed that winning the World Cup was very much achievable. Or in any of the years in which England made it to European Championships finals and all believed that England would win.

Between the lifting of the World Cup by Bobby Moore in 1966 and the failure of the so-called 'Golden Generation' 40 years later, hundreds of the best professional footballers in England shirts (and a fair few who only thought that they were the best) have universally failed to win another international trophy. That represents four decades of endless torment inflicted upon millions of England supporters doomed to watch endless replays of the only World Cup Final hat-trick in history, in lieu of any more recent successes.

England fans have had Geoff's treble rammed down their throats every time England managed to qualify for a major tournament. The film was dusted off and re-shown on TV, and in pubs and bars across the land as if to justify the ridiculous and hopeless belief that England could win. It helps to sell flags of St George and face paints in red and white, to sell programmes, inflatable cross of St George 'armchairs' and crates of German lager of course, but it doesn't help to remind everyone exactly how long ago England won anything.

Like so many followers of the game we gave to the world, and which they subsequently took to a higher plane, I have watched every England game since that fabulous day in 1966. During that lifetime I have noted the mood of England supporters change from wondering how many goals England would win by, through whether they would win, to the current condition, of wondering if they will even turn up.

This book chronicles, in results and information, photos and memories, every England team that failed in international competition between 1966 and 2006. It details the players who have starred and those who have dulled the game, and shows the success and failure rate of every manager. It also proves (as if it

The only England team to have held the real World Cup trophy (though this one was a fake) pay reverence to it on the pitch at Wembley, 30 July 1966

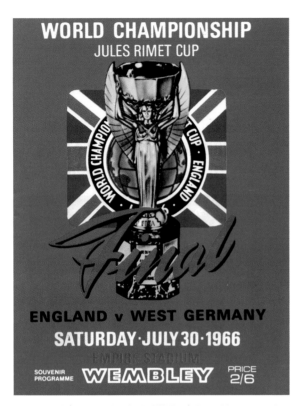

WORLD CHAMPIONSHIP
JULES RIMET CUP

Final

ENGLAND v WEST GERMANY
SATURDAY · JULY 30 · 1966
EMPIRE STADIUM
SOUVENIR PROGRAMME WEMBLEY PRICE 2/6

Programme for the World Cup Final 1966. Remind me of the score again

needed proving) how Germany, Italy, Brazil and Argentina have dominated the World Cup since 1966. And reminds us that even Denmark and Greece have won the European Championships in recent years. All England have won is the Fair Play Trophy at the Euro '96 competition in England. By the way, England have never won any competition played outside England.

It also goes some way to explaining why England have failed, and shows how it's usually been for the same reasons. While some eternal optimists can (and do) point to England's elimination from World Cups and European Championships on penalties as proof that we can be considered a top footballing nation over the 90 or 120 minutes, the fact is that basic lack of technique born of hubris has repeatedly dumped the team out of

competitions. England fans may well damn the memory of William McCrum, the Irish 'inventor' of the penalty spot in 1890, for when England lost the penalty shoot-out to Portugal in the 2006 World Cup quarter-final, it was the fifth time, in eight international tournaments over 16 years.

Coaches from Bobby Robson to Sven have told long-suffering followers of the national team that you can practise taking penalties, but you cannot replicate the pressure of a spot kick which will determine progress or elimination from a tournament. Which is true, but at least the team could practise taking penalties anyway and have a ready chosen roster of takers who were proven penalty scorers, couldn't they? Apparently not, if rumours from various England team camps are true (and they usually are), even if the players know that practise can help.

England international Matt Le Tissier, one of the many flair players who never played as many games for England as he should have (three starts between 1994–97, including an hour in a World Cup qualifier 1-0 loss to Italy, plus five sub appearances including nine minutes in a 3-0 win against Moldova), had an incredible 98% success rate in converting 49 out of 50 penalties for Southampton. He practised them regularly, he claimed, throughout his 16-year career.

So why didn't England squads on tournament duty?

That is a question that this book cannot answer, I'm afraid. It can tell you that Lee Hendrie only ever played for 14 minutes in an England shirt, during a friendly against the Czechs, under Glenn Hoddle (won 2-0), and wonder at the fact that Steve Bruce never played for England at all. But it cannot tell you why England do not practise penalties.

Failure to match the technically superior Brazilians, Portuguese, Italians, Dutch and French is kind of acceptable to careworn England fans these days (though it shouldn't be), but to find teams like the Finns, the Swedes and the Danes technically superior to England should be wholly unacceptable.

England footballers can usually be relied upon to apply work-rate, effort and determination in typical fashion in any game, but huffing and puffing without technique gets them quite simply nowhere – as the stats peppered throughout this book show.

At the 2006 World Cup England went into the tournament with the worst record for keeping possession, amongst all the finalists.

Their lack of goals has become a worrying trend since their failure in the qualifying competition for the 1974 World Cup, the 1976 European Championships and the 1978 World Cup. It was a factor in the second round of the 1982 World Cup finals when England could not muster a single goal (although they did leave the tournament unbeaten), and again at Euro '92 where England finished bottom of their group, having scored just one goal.

Between 2005 and 2007 the national team scored 19 goals in 14 matches, and of that number just seven came from strikers. Closer examination of 13 games shows that excepting the 5-0 victory over Andorra, only three goals were scored by strikers Michael Owen and Peter Crouch (2). That dismal record was made even worse by the 0-0 draw with Israel in March 2007's qualifier for the Euro 2008 finals, which equalled England's worst run for 26 years of just one goal scored in five games.

But what explains the lack of goals for England? Steven Gerrard suggested, ahead of the Euro 2008 qualifying game in Israel, that, 'You have to understand that international football is more difficult than club and Champions League football. You get a lot more chance to work on situations with your club, whereas it's bits and bobs with England.'

If England is relying on bits and bobs for goals, then

it's no wonder they struggle. But it's not only that, of course. Sven Goran Eriksson admitted after the 2002 World Cup that he had, '...found out who was a tournament player and who was not', which is great, except surely he should have known that, or at least suspected it, before going into the competition, shouldn't he? (Or maybe the FA can't afford to pay a manager with that much prescience.) And how do the FA explain that while many English players at the Euro 2004 tournament in Portugal had played in the Champions League and a World Cup too, the Greeks had fewer players with any kind of big tournament experience in their squad than possibly any other team present, and they won it?

So is lack of tournamentality a good excuse? It might have been in 1990 when England faced West Germany in the semi-final, since it was the eighth time in 10 attempts that the Germans had been in the last four and only England's second. But in 2002 or 2004?

After England beat West Germany to win the Jules Rimet Trophy in 1966, German international teams moved on and their game evolved, while England's clearly did not. Organisation became the hallmark of Teutonic football as much as technique is to Latin football and we, as a football nation, lacked both. Or rather, we mistrusted skilful technique, as the fact that Stan Bowles only won five caps, while Rodney Marsh and Tony Currie only played eight competitive matches each in the 1970s, shows. This was during the most fallow period of England's recent history, remember, and less than ten years since winning the World Cup.

So why did the English game fail to grow and develop as the international game has? Long before the trickle of overseas players into domestic football became a torrent we were warned that such an influx would be detrimental to our football, particularly the national team, and so perhaps it has come to pass.

WE ONLY LOSE TO WINNERS

Between 1972 and 2002 the team that eliminated England has gone on to win the trophy in the following competitions:

- 1970 World Cup – Brazil won the group game against England and beat West Germany in the final – who had knocked out England
- 1972 European Championships – West Germany
- 1976 European Championships – Czechoslovakia
- 1982 World Cup – West Germany (qualified from England's group)
- 1986 World Cup – Argentina
- 1988 European Championships – Holland
- 1990 World Cup – West Germany
- 1996 European Championships – Germany
- 2002 World Cup – Brazil

When the Premier League kicked off in 1992–93, there were just 11 foreign players in the newly formed top flight. However, by 2000–01, 36% of Premiership footballers were foreign and by 2004–2005 that figure was 45%. In 2007 there were 340 foreign players registered and able to appear in the Premiership. As far back as Boxing Day 1999, Chelsea became the first Premier League club to field an entirely non-English XI, at Southampton. On Valentine's Day 2005 Arsenal's first team squad of 16 for the fixture against Crystal Palace contained not a single English player.

In the early days of the Premiership the worry was that recruitment of overseas players would stop home-grown talent from progressing into first-team football. Today many Premiership academies are populated by teenagers recruited from all over the world, which means that fewer English-born youngsters get onto the books of the top teams and fail to benefit from their more advanced and better-funded training facilities. Which is why, as David Platt's report on English football points out that while the Czech Republic, Holland and

Spain have all shown improved results from their junior teams (at Under-19 and Under-21 level), the equivalent teams in England have slipped backwards in the world ratings. The Czech Republic, with a population about a fifth that of England, has overtaken our young players in results and rankings in the past ten years.

Arguably the best England player to emerge from the 2006 World Cup was Owen Hargreaves. The son of a former Bolton player who grew up in Canada, he was often lambasted for his versatility and athleticism and bemoaned as a modern-day Colin Bell, whose only use was that he could run all day. Hargreaves has been more than good enough to retain his place in the Bayern Munich side that has epitomised German football for decades, and was voted the England Supporter's Player of the Year in 2006. He made himself indispensable to England for his ability to match technique to physical effort, which he learned while playing German football, not English. In 2007 he was given the chance to bring

MOST PROLIFIC SCORERS AGAINST ENGLAND

- In June 1979 Austria scored 4 against England (who scored 3 back) in Vienna during a friendly game.
- In 1980 Wales scored 4 against England in Wrexham (England got 1) at a Home International game.
- In 2005 Denmark put 4 past David James in Copenhagen (England got 1 in return) during the friendly.
- Marco Van Basten is the only player to score a hat-trick against England since 1966. England 1 (Robson) v Holland 3 (Van Basten) at the European Championships 1988, Dusseldorf, West Germany.
- No England player since Tommy Lawton (who got 4 in an 8-2 win in Huddersfield, 1946) has scored more than 2 goals against Holland.
- (On the plus side, no German has ever scored a hat-trick against England, but Michael Owen and Geoff Hurst have both scored hat-tricks against Germany.)

Why is this man smiling?

Middlesbrough he won the League Cup (against Bolton) in 2001 and lost 'heroically' 4-0 in the final of the UEFA Cup of 2006, to Sevilla. That was it.

Then he was given the job of getting England to Euro 2008 and after beating Andorra and Macedonia, then drawing with the latter, he oversaw a loss to Croatia, England's worst defeat for 13 years. During the game Gary Neville's back pass had goalkeeper Paul Robinson kicking air and the ball bobbled into his net. 'It wasn't my fault, it was a ridiculous bobble,' bleated the Spurs keeper, continuing, 'For people to say it was an error, to say it was my fault, is ridiculous. It wasn't a mistake. I went to kick the ball and the ball wasn't there.' What did the manager have to say about the Croatian's use of a trick ball, we wonder? Or his keeper's inability to recognise when he'd made a mistake?

England then went to Israel and unimpressively drew their 'must-win' (according to McLaren) game, 0-0. The closest they came to a goal was when right-footed defender Jamie Carragher, playing at left back, headed against the bar. In the aftermath of yet another dismal England performance, at Steve McLaren's post-match interview, his first words when asked where do we go from here were, 'We keep going and do the same things.' You could almost hear David Platt's snort of derision a thousand miles away. (In the post-match press conference McLaren said to the downhearted assembled English Press, 'We've only lost a football match.' Which they hadn't, of course.)

That result gave McClaren an unenviable record, of the worst start to a tenure by any of England's 11 full-time managers. Nor did it get much better in the next game against Andorra (ranked 163rd in the world), when England struggled for three-quarters of the game. Steven Gerrard (2) and Championship striker David Nugent, marking his debut as the first Preston player capped by England for 50 years, scored to win the game but worryingly England won due to their superior

those skills to England, in the Man Utd midfield.

The English work ethic as epitomised by Hargreaves, and used to such good effect by Ramsey, should be the foundation upon which technique can be built, not used as a substitute for that technique. All young English players need is the chance to do just that, and by playing at a high enough level to learn it properly, from managers who can impart the right kind of advice.

Which begs the question of whether Steve McLaren has the ability to do any of that. As a club manager with fitness, and not their ability.

With qualification to Euro 2008 hanging in the balance at the time of writing, it has to be hoped that the FA read and digest David Platt's report on the game and how it could and should develop.

If there is to be improvement in technique and ability, as Platt points out, the emphasis has got to be on developing better skills and their implementation at a young age (he says eight). That way there is more likelihood of individual skill transcending team play when, as has often been the case with England, team play falls down.

Football is imbedded in English popular culture but it must be remembered that footballers are a product of their generation, and we are seeing a wholly different one to those which produced Stanley Matthews, Jimmy Greaves, Bobby Charlton and Gary Lineker. They were once kids who bounced a tennis ball against the kerb or dribbled over cobbled streets to improve control and technique. Today those kids are playing at being Kaka or Ronaldo on computers, sitting stationary and with a virtual football. They need to be enticed outside, onto pitches with human coaches who can inspire them and teach them how to be world beaters.

It would also help enormously if fans and the media who feed them so much hyperbolic nonsense gave in and accepted that maybe our players are not quite as good as we, and they, are led to believe.

If we accept that England are not going to win anything there's always the chance that we could be pleasantly surprised. So stop assuming that England will win a trophy. Even if they progress to the latter stages of a World Cup or a European Championships, do not presume that England will win a penalty shoot-out, let alone the Final. Set yourself free.

Hopefully then the FA can then get on with aiding the development of a team who stand a genuine chance of competing at the highest level.

P.S. For future reference, if England manage to win the World Cup in 2010 (or even qualify for it), check out how many players below feature in that success:

ENGLAND'S FUTURE DREAMING	
POSITION	CLUB AS OF JUNE 2007
GOALKEEPERS:	
Ben Foster	Man Utd
Scott Carson	Liverpool
Chris Kirkland	Wigan Athletic
DEFENDERS:	
Justin Hoyte	Arsenal
Micah Richards	Man City
Ashley Cole	Chelsea
John Terry	Chelsea
Jonathan Woodgate	Middlesbrough
Michael Dawson	Tottenham
MIDFIELD	
Owen Hargreaves	Man Utd
Steven Gerrard	Liverpool
Aaron Lennon	Tottenham
Theo Walcott	Arsenal
Scott Sinclair	Chelsea
Joe Cole	Chelsea
Giles Barnes	Derby County
David Bentley	Blackburn Rovers
Tom Huddlestone	Tottenham
FORWARDS	
Michael Owen	Newcastle Utd
Wayne Rooney	Man Utd
Dean Ashton	West Ham
David Nugent	Preston North End
Michael Chopra	Cardiff City

The official dinner for the World Champions 1966. L-R (as listed on the original photo) Bobby Charlton, Mrs Charlton, Bobby Moore, Mrs Moore, Tonia Ramsey (daughter), Alf Ramsey, Mrs Ramsey, Mrs Hurst, Geoff Hurst. In front of them is the real Jules Rimet Trophy, The one behind them is fake

WORLD CUP ENGLAND 1966

'OUR GOLDEN BOYS!' [DAILY MAIL]

It was only 21 years since WWII had ended and London was still scarred by bombsites. Men and women who had fought for their freedom wore suits and hats to work. The media may have thought that London was 'Swinging', but in truth all the swinging was being done in just a few clubs and boutiques on the Kings Road. For most of the population, England in 1966 was not so very different from the place it had been when the War ended. The Festival of Britain in 1951 had been devised to cheer up a nation of people who were still suffering from rationing, but they didn't really take to the enormous concrete bunker built on London's South Bank. The 'new' Queen's coronation in 1953 was a day off, but really, apart from Winston Churchill's funeral in 1965, England hadn't seen much in the way of internationally renowned pomp and splendour since May 1945.

For those who were not around at the time it is impossible to understate the impact that the staging of the World Cup finals in England had on the country. Especially to football fans. Up to that point Pelé was someone only read about and rarely seen, football games on the telly were restricted to the FA Cup final or occasional European games and then in grainy black and white images.

There was a genuine sense of keen anticipation at grounds from Liverpool (Goodison) to Birmingham (Villa Park) and Manchester (Old Trafford) to London (Wembley) as they prepared to play host to Pak Doo Ik, Eusebio, Emmerich, Beckenbauer and football's first true global superstar, Edson Arantes do Nascimento, or Pelé as he was more commonly known.

The World Cup of 1958 had made the then 17-year-old Brazilian a star – he scored the only goal against Wales and a hat-trick against France in the semi-final before helping his team to carry away the trophy. And since the Brazilians had also won the 1962 World Cup, their visit to England added a glamour to the

Still the only hat-trick in a World Cup final: Hurst gets his third

competition. Most people thought that Brazil would win it again, at Wembley.

It may be odd to consider now but no-one in England expected the home nation to win the trophy. When Alf Ramsey, who had followed Walter Winterbottom into the job of England manager after turning Ipswich into a major League force, claimed that 'England will win the World Cup', he became the subject of much derision.

Because they were to be the hosts, England had not played competitive games leading up to the finals. Manager Ramsey made his seminal decision to abandon wingers well before the summer finals, in the aftermath of a 3-2 reverse to Austria, which was only the third time England had lost to foreign opposition on home soil. In December 1965 England went to Madrid and with a 4-3-3 formation defeated the reigning European Champions 2-0. Significantly, Alan Ball tucked in to replace a conventional right winger and Bobby Charlton dropped in from left winger to play deep behind the strikers. Nine of the team that beat Spain would play in the World Cup final seven months later.

However, with just one defeat in 21 matches going into the finals (and of the finalists only Hungary had

ENGLAND SQUAD

	CLUB	AGE	CAPS	GOALS
GOALKEEPERS				
Gordon Banks	Leicester	28	27	
Ron Springett	Sheff Wed	30	32	
Peter Bonetti	Chelsea	24	1	
FULL BACKS				
George Cohen	Fulham	26	24	
Ray Wilson	Everton	31	45	
Jimmy Armfield	Blackpool	30	42	
Gerry Byrne	Liverpool	28	2	
CENTRE BACKS				
Jack Charlton	Leeds	30	16	2
Bobby Moore	West Ham	25	41	2
Ron Flowers	Wolves	31	49	10
Norman Hunter	Leeds	22	4	
MIDFIELD				
Alan Ball	Blackpool	21	10	1
Norbert Stiles	Man Utd	24	14	1
Bobby Charlton	Man Utd	28	68	40
Martin Peters	West Ham	22	3	1
George Eastham	Arsenal	29	19	2
FORWARDS				
John Connelly	Man Utd	28	19	7
Terry Paine	S'hampton	27	18	7
Ian Callaghan	Liverpool	24	1	
Roger Hunt	Liverpool	27	13	12
Geoff Hurst	West Ham	24	5	1
Jimmy Greaves	Tottenham	26	51	43

Previous page: BACK L-R: Cocker, Cohen, Byrne, Hunt, Flowers, Banks, Springett, Bonetti, Greaves, Moore, Connelly, Eastham, Shepherdson. MIDDLE L-R: Armfield, Stiles, Charlton J, Hurst, Paine, Wilson, Peters, Ball, Charlton R. FRONT L-R: Hunter, Callaghan

THE MANAGER: ALF RAMSEY

Alf began his playing career at Southampton in 1946 and moved to Tottenham in 1949, where over five years he scored 24 goals in 276 appearances, from full back. He helped Spurs to the Second Division title in 1950, and the First Division Championship the following season. He won 32 England caps following his debut against Switzerland in December 1948, with 29 of them in consecutive internationals. He scored three times, all from penalties.

Ipswich Town appointed him manager in 1955 and he won the Third Division (South) in 1957, the Second Division title in 1961 and the First Division title in 1962. He was the first to win First and Second Division titles as both player and manager. While manager at Portman Road, Ramsey perfected his wingless wonders formation, preferring to play a deep-lying forward in the hole behind the strikers.

Ramsey became England manager in May 1963, and insisted on having full powers of team selection, something that had been the domain of the FA Committee since 1872. In effect he became the first, true England manager. His reign began with a 5-2 defeat in France. For the next game, against Scotland in spring of 1964, Ron Springett the goalkeeper was replaced by Gordon Banks. England lost again (0-1), but they won the next four in a row as Ramsey bedded in new players – including a 4-3 victory in Lisbon against Portugal and a 10-0 trouncing of the USA in New York.

Between his first game and the realisation of his prophecy that England would win the World Cup, the national team played a total of 44 games and won 29 of them.

England didn't lose a match for nearly two years between 1965 and 1967. If those results were equated to the 42-game First Division programme of the day, they would have given England the League Championship each season.

RAMSEY'S ENGLAND RECORD 1963–1966 WORLD CUP FINAL

P	W	D	L	F	A	WIN %
44	29	9	6	106	52	65.9

NORMAN HUNTER. Although Hunter was a tough tackling defender, very much like Ramsey had been, he wasn't really a Ramsey kind of player. There were far more experienced members of the squad who could do the same job as the Leeds man. Jimmy Armfield, who had been voted the best right back in the previous World Cup, for instance, or Ron Flowers, who had a pretty decent scoring record for a centre back/wing half. He was not needed, but was there.

JOHN 'BUDGIE' BYRNE is one of only five players to be capped while playing in the Third Division (with Crystal Palace), and ended up scoring eight goals in 11 games after his non-scoring debut against Northern Ireland in 1961. He scored two in his next game against Switzerland, even though it was two years later, in June 1963. Budgie was discarded by Ramsey a year before the World Cup finals, despite being Hurst's striking partner at West Ham.

ever beaten England at home), the bookies made Ramsey's men second favourites, behind holders Brazil. Mainly to attract the punters' money whatever the odds, it has to be argued.

The tournament's opening game between the hosts and Uruguay did little to raise the odds on England winning the Cup. It was one of the most boring games ever staged at Wembley, and ended 0-0 with the only excitement in the game being supplied by Nobby Stiles.

His punch at Rocha was not the most violent action on the pitch, but it was certainly the most theatrical.

England met Mexico next, knowing a win would secure a quarter-final berth. Bobby Charlton scored England's first goal of the World Cup in his usual spectacular fashion. Hunt unselfishly created space for the United man and his 25-yard thunderbolt hit the back of the net before Calderon hit the deck from his despairing dive. Roger Hunt later tapped home a second and England were through.

With qualification assured, France were the opposition in the final group game. Just before half time Hunt was on hand to turn in a rebound after Jack Charlton headed against the post. Fifteen minutes from time Hunt scored again. England won the group to earn a third World Cup quarter-final and for the third time faced South American opponents in Argentina.

'ANIMALS!' (ALF RAMSEY)

Before that game, Ramsey threatened to resign if his bosses at the FA insisted that he couldn't play Nobby Stiles against Argentina. Nobby had been called The Beast by the French media after poleaxing Simon in the last group match and the FA thought that he'd been 'ungentlemanly' in his crunching tackle. Forty years later the FA wouldn't know a gentleman if he tipped his bowler to their collective faces of course, but back then decorum was of the utmost importance to the men who ran the Association. Luckily for Nobby, Alf, and the whole nation, they backed down on their demand for Stiles' removal from the team and he went on to prove essential for one of the roughest games ever played by England.

With Jimmy Greaves suffering a gashed shin from the French game, it fell to Geoff Hurst, a former wing half, to fill in for the greatest goalscorer in English

football. And with Ramsey plumping for a flexible 4-4-2 into 4-3-3 formation with Hurst and Hunt up front being joined by Charlton or Peters when possible, Ramsey's 'wingless wonders' were born.

The game was littered with niggling fouls exacerbated by South American petulance. The Argentinian captain Rattin was the most verbal transgressor and unfortunately he upset the referee Mr Kreitlein (of West Germany) so much that just before the intervals, he was sent off. Rattin refused to go and it took nine minutes and a FIFA official's intervention before the captain went into the record books as the second player to be sent off at Wembley.

With 12 minutes remaining, West Ham's Hurst steered the perfect header home from a Peters cross to earn a first ever World Cup semi-final place for England. Alf Ramsey did himself and his country little credit with his post-match pronouncement that Argentina 'acted like animals', especially since England were guilty of 33 fouls to the South American's 19, but few people in England seemed to notice or care.

Leading up to the semi-final, England had won 10 and drawn the other in 11 matches, with only one goal conceded in nine games. It was their best sequence of results for more than 50 years.

Ramsey announced an unchanged line-up for the

semi, which meant Hurst instead of Greaves. The game was originally to be played at Goodison Park, but was switched to Wembley since the national stadium could hold more spectators. And so 88,000 people witnessed a fantastic exhibition of flowing football from both England and Portugal. While Eusebio's late penalty was the first goal conceded by Gordon Banks in the competition, it came after a Bobby Charlton brace had ensured that England went to the final.

That they were to face West Germany meant England were slight favourites, since they had won the previous seven meetings between them. Ramsey named an unchanged side again, consigning Greaves to a footnote in English football history and putting Geoff Hurst into the record books.

The great Portuguese forward Eusebio salutes the crowd

The hottest ticket of the last 40 years

'THEY THINK IT'S ALL OVER' (KENNETH WOLSTENHOLME)

The first goal of the final took only 12 minutes to arrive. Haller took advantage of the first mistake anyone could recall being made by Ray Wilson in the finals, to put West Germany ahead. Those watching on television were reminded by commentator Ken Wolstenholme that in every final since the War the team that scored first had lost.

Six minutes later, Bobby Moore flighted a wonderful free-kick into the penalty box for Hurst to steer a headed equaliser past Tilkowski. Parity spurred England on and when Peters stabbed England ahead,

WORLD CUP 1966 RESULTS

GROUP 1 WINNERS: ENGLAND
England P3/W2/D1/L0/F4/A0
England 0 v Uruguay 0
11 July 1966 (Wembley)
England 2 [Charlton R, Hunt] v Mexico 0
16 July 1966 (Wembley)
England 2 [Hunt (2)] v France 0
20 July 1966 (Wembley)

QUARTER-FINAL
England 1 [Hurst] v Argentina 0
23 July 1966 (Wembley)

SEMI-FINAL
England 2 [Charlton R (2)] v Portugal 1 [Eusebio]
26 July 1966 (Wembley)

THE FINAL
England 4 [Hurst (3), Peters] v W Germany 2 [Haller, Weber] AET (2-2)
30 July 1966 (Wembley)

13 minutes from time, the nation held its collective breath until, seconds from party-time, Jack Charlton conceded a foul to Held. When Emmerich fired the subsequent free-kick through the England wall, Wolfgang Weber swooped to steer home at the far post in the 89th minute.

Into extra-time the most contentious goal scored in a World Cup Final put England ahead in the 101st minute. For 40 years Germans have contested it as not a goal. For 40 years English supporters have clung to the opposite view. Even the advent of digital technology has failed to verify what linesman Takrim Bakhramov ordained with only his eyesight. Namely that Hurst's shot, after hitting the bar, HAD crossed the line. Ken Wolstenholme insisted years later that, 'The crossbar was elliptical and when the ball came down it spun behind the line before hitting the line.' Which must have been what the Russian linesman thought.

The award of the goal deflated the Germans and in the 120th minute Hurst burst forward, 'with people on the pitch' as Wolstenholme commented, to smack the ball home to make it 4-2. The Jules Rimet Trophy was staying in England for the next four years. And let no-one forget that Hurst's hat-trick, the only final triple ever, was THE perfect treble, being from a right-foot shot, a left-foot shot and a header.

Several decades later it emerged that between the presentation by the Queen to Bobby Moore and Stiles' jig around Wembley, the trophy was replaced with a replica. Not that it mattered to Nobby or the nation as a whole, of course. Today that replica is permanently displayed at the National Football Museum, in Preston. Which is a good thing, as Brazil lost the original after they were awarded it for the third and final time, following their 1970 triumph.

And so it was that England's football glory came on the afternoon of 30 July 1966. As successive generations of English footballers to have represented their country in competitions since will tell you, it was the worst thing that ever happened to the game...

EUROPEAN CHAMPIONSHIPS ITALY 1968

'WE ARE THE WORLD CHAMPIONS'

(THE *SCOTSMAN*)

Just two years after their home triumph at the World Cup, Ramsey's Heroes entered the recently renamed European Football Championships for the second time. Qualification to the two-game finals (the semi-final, third place play-off or final), to be held in Italy in June 1968, was decided on the aggregate of results from the Home Internationals of 1967 and 1968.

In anticipation of English fans and press expectancy, Sir Alf (he was knighted in 1967) had begun rebuilding his team almost immediately after the World Cup win. Alan Mullery replaced Stiles because as well as being a similar hard-tackling player he also scored goals. George Cohen made way for Keith Newton, who could play in either full back berth, and having completely discarded Jimmy Greaves, Ramsey settled on Hurst and Hunt as his main strikers.

Having won the 1967–68 Home Internationals competition, England lined up against Spain in a two-legged quarter-final at Wembley and grabbed a 1-0 win thanks to Bobby Charlton. Significantly perhaps, Sir Alf did not predict that England would win the Championships either before or after the game.

In Madrid a defensively minded England line-up secured a surprise 2-1 win, with goals from Peters and Norman Hunter. England were set for a semi-final date with Yugoslavia, in Florence in June.

In a physically testing game neither goalkeeper was really stretched, although Yugoslavia looked the more threatening side. It was always possible that one goal would settle the tie, and it came after the sending-off of Alan Mullery, in the second half.

Sir Alf Ramsey puts his players through their paces in training. Note the lack of cigarettes in hands. Sir Alf was a stickler for a healthy routine

ENGLAND SQUAD

	CLUB	AGE	CAPS	GOALS
GOALKEEPERS				
Gordon Banks	Stoke City	30	41	
Alex Stepney	Man Utd	25	n/a	
Gordon West	Everton	25	n/a	
FULL BACKS				
Keith Newton	Blackburn	26	7	
Ray Wilson	Everton	33	59	
Cyril Knowles	Tottenham	23	1	
Tommy Wright	Everton	23	0	
CENTRE BACKS				
Bobby Moore	West Ham	26	57	2
Brian Labone	Everton	28	6	
Jack Charlton	Leeds	32	27	4
Norman Hunter	Leeds	24	5	
MIDFIELDERS				
Alan Mullery	Tottenham	26	7	
Martin Peters	West Ham	24	16	6
Alan Ball	Everton	22	23	4
Bobby Charlton	Man Utd	30	82	43
Nobby Stiles	Man Utd	25	24	1
Colin Bell	Man City	22	2	
FORWARDS				
Roger Hunt	Liverpool	29	27	17
Geoff Hurst	West Ham	26	18	9
Mike Summerbee	Man City	25	1	
Jimmy Greaves	Tottenham	28	57	44
Peter Thompson	Liverpool	25	13	

Previous page: L-R BACK: Shepherson, Greaves, Eastham, Callaghan, Hurst, Thompson, Hunter, Springett, Hunt, Charlton R, Connolly, Milne, Newton, Armfield, Moore. FRONT L-R: Banks, Knowles, Bonetti, Flowers, Cohen, Charlton J, Peters, Byrne, Swan, Paine, Ball, Stiles

THE MANAGER: SIR ALF RAMSEY

In winning the 1966 World Cup Alf Ramsey secured for himself the title of most successful England manager ever. Throw in his record as national manager, making him one of only two England managers to boast a win ratio better than 60%, and it's a CV that will remain unsurpassed for some time. He was knighted in the 1967 New Years Honours list (his captain Bobby Moore received an OBE in the same list), picking up the gong at Buckingham Palace before his England team lost their first match as World Champions.

That defeat came in April 1967, at Wembley, and against the auld enemy, Scotland. The Scots claimed then (and ever since, of course) that the victory made them the true World Champions, using as proof the fact that the England team they faced lined up almost exactly as they had done against the Germans in 1966, but with the exception of Greaves for Hunt. The Scots, of course, insisted that it was a stronger team than faced the Germans because of that change.

According to Denis Law (who scored the first goal that day), the 2-3 scoreline flattered England, and had the Scots' central midfield wizard Jim Baxter pushed the ball forward to score goals, rather than use it to humiliate the English players, it could well have been 5 or 6 to the Scots.

Forty years later Law recalled screaming, 'Let's give them a doing!' to Baxter, who just smiled and replied, 'Naw. let's just take the piss out of them' before playing 'piggy in the middle' with Billy Bremner and Tommy Gemmell using Alan Ball as the scurrying little piggy. Infuriatingly for Ramsey, the other defeat that England suffered between winning the World Cup and the Euro '68 semi-final against Yugoslavia, was a 1-0 friendly loss to the West Germans in Hanover four days before the semi. Franz Beckenbauer getting the only goal in the first game between the teams since Hurst's hat-trick.

RAMSEY'S ENGLAND RECORD 31 JULY 1966 – 2 JUNE 1968

P	W	D	L	F	A	WIN %
14	9	3	2	26	10	64

WHY WAS HE THERE?

MIKE SUMMERBEE. A winger, he played against Spain in the first leg of the quarter-final, but had to wait another four years for his next cap. Although a part of the most successful Man City team ever, Summerbee was a practical joker who also had a very short temper. So he was easily riled and liked to play tricks on teammates. Which suggests that he would be exactly the kind of player to annoy Sir Alf. His presence in the squad seems more baffling when you consider that at no point did a newspaper demand his inclusion.

WHY WASN'T HE THERE?

JIMMY GREAVES won the last of his 57 caps in the 1-0 win over Austria in May 1967, after scoring his 44th England goal in a friendly versus Spain three days earlier. Jimmy never went to the semi-finals but after England's failure there was a media campaign, with strong public support, for Greaves' reinstatement. Unfortunately, Sir Alf Ramsey preferred hard running forwards who subscribed to the work ethic and intuitive flair players, like Greaves, who operated on instinct, had no place in his team.

The Spurs man had just been the victim of a late tackle by Trivic but his retaliation ensured that Mullery made history by becoming the first England player to be sent off in a full international match. Trivic jumped to his feet immediately that Mullery walked. The cry of 'those dastardly foreigners' went up at houses and in clubs across England as their national team's 10 men went on to struggle with the mobile Yugoslav attack.

Our brave boys almost made it to the end of the game and an outcome that would be decided by the toss of a coin (as did the other semi-final between Italy and Russia), but the match winner came just four minutes from the end of the game.

Dragan Dzajic capitalised when Bobby Moore failed to judge a spinning cross correctly, and he fired past Banks. However, England did go on to win the Third

ABOVE: An original programme for the 1968 European Championships finals in Italy

RIGHT: Bobby Moore leads out the world champions against Spain in the home leg of the Euro Championships quarter-final

MOST DANGEROUS ENGLAND PLAYER

MARTIN PETERS. There was enough goal power in the England squad in Italy but it never clicked into action until it was too late. However, Peters was England's most dangerous player with a scoring record of six goals in 16 internationals prior to the game against Spain and eight goals in 19 games before meeting Yugoslavia.

MOST DANGEROUS OPPONENT

DRAGAN DZAJIC of Yugoslavia caused endless problems in the semi-final and scored the only goal of the game. He proved it wasn't a one-off either as he opened the scoring in the final against Italy, who went on to equalise and the game was drawn. Italy won the replay (there were no penalties in 1968).

MOST OVERRATED ENGLAND PLAYER

ROGER HUNT bore the brunt of fans' dissatisfaction after the European Championships. The Liverpool striker had a terrific scoring record for his country but didn't hit the net in Italy. Early in 1969, as the campaign to restore Greaves to the national team gathered momentum in the media, Hunt asked Ramsey not to select him again.

Place match, 2-0 against USSR (who lost the toss in their semi-final), with goals from Bobby Charlton and Geoff Hurst.

The post-tournament inquiries into England's deficiencies by the media were tame in comparison to later outbursts, but echoed those that were about to accompany every competitive outing for England.

It was only two years since the Great Triumph, but England were most definitely expecting better things than third place. Little did they know that even third place was to become a mere dream when faced with tricky, technically superior and devious opponents.

EUROPEAN CHAMPIONSHIPS 1968

GROUP 8 WINNERS: ENGLAND

England P6/W4/D1/L1/F15/A5
N. Ireland 0 v England 2 [Hunt, Peters]
20 Oct 1966 (Belfast)
England 5 [Hurst (2), Charlton R, Hennessy (o.g.), Charlton J] v Wales 1 [Davies]
16 Nov 1966 (Wembley)
England 2 [Charlton J, Hurst] v Scotland 3 [Law, McCalliog, Lennox]
15 April 1967 (Wembley)
Wales 0 v England 3 [Peters, Charlton R, Ball]
21 Oct 1967 (Cardiff)
England 2 [Hurst, Charlton R] v N. Ireland 0
22 Nov 1967 (Wembley)
Scotland 1 [Hughes] v England 1 [Peters]
24 Feb 1968 (Glasgow)

QUARTER-FINAL 1ST LEG

England 1 [Charlton R] v Spain 0
3 April 1968 (Wembley)
Spain 1 [Armancio] v England 2 [Peters, Hunter]
8 May 1968 (Madrid)

SEMI-FINAL

England 0 v Yugoslavia 1 [Dzajic]
5 June 1968 (Florence)

THIRD PLACE PLAY-OFF

England 2 [Charlton R, Hurst] v USSR 0
8 June 1968 (Rome 3pm)

THE FINAL

Italy 1 [Domenghini] v Yugoslavia 1 [Dzajic]
8 June 1968 (Rome 9.15pm)
Replay: Italy 2 [Riva, Anastasi] v Yugoslavia 0
10 June 1968 (Rome)

ENGLAND'S NIGHTMARE OPPONENTS

There are three teams that England have had the most trouble beating in competitions since 1966. They are Brazil, Portugal and, most often, Germany.

Germany (and pre-1991, West Germany) are England's nightmare opponents. Even Wembley hasn't given any advantage to the English team: they have won only one of the five games played there between the teams since 1966, with the Germans winning the other four. Since the 1966 World Cup final, England have played the Germans 17 times in competitive and friendly games, winning only four to their nine.

Since the same date, it's been two English victories to the Portuguese four, and two to the Brazilian seven.

ENGLAND V PORTUGAL (POST-30 JULY 1966)
P12/W2/D6/L4/F12/A10
THE GAMES
England 1 [Charlton J] v Portugal 0
10 Dec 1969 (Wembley) Friendly
Portugal 0 v England 0
4 April 1974 (Lisbon, Portugal) Friendly
England 0 v Portugal 0
20 Nov 1974 (Wembley) European Championships qualifier
Portugal 1 [Rodrigues] v England 1 [Channon]
19 Nov 1975 (Lisbon) European Championships qualifier
Portugal 1 [Correia] v England 0
3 June 1986 (Monterrey, Mexico) World Cup Group F
England 1 [Stone] v Portugal 1 [Alves]
12 Dec 1995 (Wembley) Friendly
England 3 [Shearer (2), Sheringham] v Portugal 0
22 April 1998 (Wembley) Friendly
England 2 [McManaman, Scholes] v Portugal 3 [Figo, Pinto, Gomes]
12 June 2000 (Eindhoven, Holland) Euro Championships Group A
England 1 [Smith] v Portugal 1 [Costinha]
7 Sept 2002 (Villa Park, England) Friendly
Portugal 1 [Resendes] v England 1 [King]
18 Feb 2004 (Faro, Portugal) Friendly
Portugal 2 [Costa, Postiga] v England 2 [Owen, Lampard] *6-5 pen, AET
24 June 2004 (Lisbon) Euro Championships quarter-final
England 0 v Portugal 0 *1-3 pen, aet
1 July 2006 (Gelsenkirchen, Germany) World Cup quarter-final

The sight that no English fan can stand to look at for too long: German captain Franz Beckenbauer lifts the World Cup in 1974. (Their second.)

ENGLAND V BRAZIL (POST-30 JULY 1966)

P16/W2/D7/L7/F12/A16

THE GAMES

Brazil 2 [Goncalves, Ventura] v England 1 [Bell]

12 June 1969 (Maracana, Brazil) Friendly

England 0 v Brazil 1 [Jairzinho]

7 June 1970 (Guadalajara, Mexico) World Cup Group C

Brazil 1 [de Oliveira] v England 0

23 May 1976 (Los Angeles, USA) US Bi-Centennial Tournament

Brazil 0 v England 0

8 June 1977 (Maracana, Brazil) Friendly

England 1 [Keegan] v Brazil 1 [Alves]

19 April 1978 (Wembley) Friendly

England 0 v Brazil 1 [Antunes]

12 July 1981 (Wembley) Friendly

Brazil 0 v England 2 [Barnes J, Hateley]

10 June 1984 (Maracana, Brazil) Friendly

England 1 [Lineker] v Brazil 1 [Lima]

19 May 1987 (Wembley) Rous Cup

England 1 [Lineker] v Brazil 0

28 Mar 1990 (Wembley) Friendly

England 1 [Platt] v Brazil 1 [de Gama]

17 May 1992 (Wembley) Friendly

England 1 [Platt] v Brazil 1 [Santos]

13 June 1993 (Washington DC, USA) US Cup

England 1 [Le Saux] v Brazil 3 [Junior, de Lima, Alves]

11 June 1995 (Wembley) Umbro Int. Tournament

England 0 v Brazil 1 [de Souza]

10 June 1997 (Paris, France) Tournoi de France

England 1 [Owen] v Brazil 1 [Sena]

27 May 2000 (Wembley) Friendly

England 1 [Owen] v Brazil 2 [Rivaldo, Ronaldinho]

21 June 2002 (Shizuoka, Japan) World Cup quarter-final

England 1 [Terry] v Brazil 1 [Diego]

1 June 2007 (Wembley) Friendly

ENGLAND V GERMANY (POST-30 JULY 1966)

P17/W4/D4/L9/F20/A21

THE GAMES

W Germany 1 [Beckenbauer] v England 0

1 June 1968 (Hanover, West Germany) Friendly

W Germany 3 [Beckenbauer, Seeler, Muller] v England 2 [Mullery, Peters]

14 June 1970 (Leon, Mexico) World Cup quarter-final

England 1 [Lee] v W Germany 3 [Hoeness, Netzer (pen), Muller]

29 April 1972 (Wembley) Euro qualifier

W Germany 0 v England 0

13 May 1972 (Berlin, East Germany) Euro qualifier

England 2 [Bell, MacDonald] v W Germany 0

12 Mar 1975 (Wembley) Friendly

W Germany 2 [Worm, Bonhoff] v England 1 [Pearson]

22 Feb 1978 (Munich, West Germany)

W Germany 0 v England 0

29 June 1982 (Madrid, Spain) World Cup 2nd round

England 1 [Woodcock] v W Germany 2 [Rummenigge 2]

13 Oct 1982 (Wembley) Friendly

England 3 [Dixon K (2), Robson] v W Germany 0

12 June 1985 (Mexico City, Mexico) Azteca 2000 Tournament

W Germany 3 [Litbarski (2), Wuttke] v England 1 [Lineker]

9 Sept 1987 (Dusseldorf, West Germany) Friendly

W Germany 1 [Brehme] v England 1 [Lineker] *4-3 pen, AET

4 July 1990 (Turin, Italy) World Cup semi-final

England 0 v Germany 1 [Riedle]

11 Sept 1991 (Wembley) Friendly

England 1 [Shearer] v Germany 1 [Kuntz] *5-6 pen, AET

26 June 1996 (Wembley) Euro Championships semi-final

England 1 [Shearer] v Germany 0

20 June 2000 (Charleroi, France) Euro Championships Group A

England 0 v Germany 1 [Hamman]

7 Oct 2000 (Wembley) World Cup qualifier

Germany 1 [Jancker] v England 5 [Owen (3), Gerrard, Heskey]

1 Sept 2001 (Munich, Germany) World Cup qualifier

WORLD CUP MEXICO 1970

'THOUGH THEY THINK WE'RE THE GREATEST'

('BACK HOME', THE OFFICIAL ENGLAND POP SONG 1970)

Mexico '70 was the first World Cup to be broadcast in colour. The gold of the Brazilian strip contrasted beautifully with the azure blue of the Italian in what many consider to be the best final ever contested — certainly the final goal, by Carlos Alberto, is universally considered the best one scored in any World Cup. Tellingly, the best remembered contribution to the spectacle in Mexico from the English was a magnificent save (likewise regarded by many as the best ever) by Gordon Banks from a Pelé header. That, and the disappearing trick that Bobby Moore was supposed to have pulled off with a bracelet in a jewellers on a pre-tournament trip to Bogotá, Colombia. If the false accusation of theft was designed to ruffle the cool of the reigning World Champions' captain, it failed. Little bothered Mooro. Sadly, the same could not be said of England's goalscorers. They managed a paltry four goals in four games – one of which was a penalty and another by a defender. Plus, for the first time under Sir Alf's management, England lost a two-goal lead in a competitive game, and were eliminated by West Germany in the quarter-finals.

'WE'LL GIVE ALL WE'VE GOT TO GIVE' ('BACK HOME')

England's World Cup began bathed in sunlight and shadow from a mysterious, huge star-shaped object

Pre-kick-off v Brazil, 7 June 1970 L-R: Peters, Hurst, Labone, Cooper, Banks, Mullery, Lee, Ball, Wright, Charlton, Moore

ENGLAND SQUAD

	CLUB	AGE	CAPS	GOALS
GOALKEEPERS				
Gordon Banks	Stoke City	32	59	
Peter Bonetti	Chelsea	28	6	
Alex Stepney	Man Utd	25	1	
DEFENDERS				
Terry Cooper	Leeds	25	8 -	
Emlyn Hughes	Liverpool	22	6	
Keith Newton	Everton	28	23	
Tommy Wright	Everton	25	9	
Jack Charlton	Leeds	35	34	6
Norman Hunter	Leeds	26	13	1
Brian Labone	Everton	30	23	
Bobby Moore	West Ham	29	80	2
MIDFIELD				
Alan Ball	Blackpool	25	41	6
Colin Bell	Man City	24	11	2
Bobby Charlton	Man Utd	32	102	49
Alan Mullery	Tottenham	28	27	
Martin Peters	Tottenham	26	38	14
Nobby Stiles	Man Utd	28	28	1
FORWARDS				
Jeff Astle	West Brom	28	3	
Allan Clarke	Leeds	23	-	
Geoff Hurst	West Ham	28	38	20
Francis Lee	Man City	26	14	6
Peter Osgood	Chelsea	23	1	-

Previous page: L-R BACK: Osgood, Kidd, Hughes, Charlton R, Bonetti, Clarke, Unknown. 2nd ROW L-R: Shilton, unknown, Newton, Thompson, Bell. 3rd ROW L-R: Shepherdson, Stiles, Lee, Coates, Cocker, Cooper, unknown, Ball, Hunter. FRONT L-R: Labone, Hurst, Stepney, Banks, Moore, Charlton J, Astle, Mullery, Peters

THE MANAGER: SIR ALF RAMSEY

As reward for winning the World Cup in 1966, only the manager and captain had had any kind of official recognition for their achievement. In fact, no other player was officially recognised for the small part they played in the game, for some years to come. They went to Mexico with the words of their modestly triumphal pop single ringing in their ears. Like the manager, it was quietly positive and stated that the players were ever mindful of the supporters 'Back Home'. Sir Alf had confidently led England to their first European Championships finals, in 1968, and looked bemused when they finished third (see page 24).

As holders of the World Cup, England didn't have to qualify for Mexico '70, so had to play as many meaningful friendlies as possible in order for the manager to try out some new talent. Jeff Astle, Ian Storey-Moore, Peter Osgood, Brian Kidd, Ralph Coates and Emlyn Hughes all won first caps in 1969 or '70, although only Astle and Osgood were to travel to Mexico. Allan Clarke made his debut in the World Cup.

Mexico '70 wasn't great for Sir Alf. He refused the use of a Spanish-speaking aid (who could have helped no end in the jewellers in Bogotá alone) before flying out and failed to tell the players that he would lose six of them from the squad just before the competition began; they learned of their omission via the media first. His autocratic style was accepted by players and the FA as long as his team was successful, of course. But when he made the mistake of removing Bobby Charlton against West Germany his tactical nous was called into doubt for the first, but not last, time.

RAMSEY'S ENGLAND RECORD 2 JUNE 1968 – 1970 WORLD CUP

P	W	D	L	F	A	WIN %
20	12	7	1	36	11	60

JEFF ASTLE was an old-fashioned English centre forward. Good in the air and good in the box against lumbering English centre halves, he just wasn't international quality. He scored no goals in his five internationals, all except one of which were quite important. He's now best remembered for his miss against Brazil after coming on as a substitute. He never played again for England after the final group game against Czechoslovakia.

ALAN HUDSON was just 20 in 1970 and Ramsey had stated publicly that he was tempted to take him to Mexico. Yet he then had to wait five years for his England debut. There's little doubt he was technically more skilled and adept than any of the midfielders England did take to Mexico in defence of the Jules Rimet trophy. Maybe it was the length of his hair that put Sir Alf off. He won only two caps, both under Don Revie, both wins – one against West Germany.

cast onto the pitch, on a late afternoon in Guadalajara. Geoff Hurst began where he'd left off in 1966, turning in a cross from Ball just past the hour. Bobby Charlton went close to scoring, but one was enough for a win.

The next game saw a meeting between the teams who'd won the last three World Cups. England lost the game, thanks to the BBC. Their group game against Brazil was played in the stifling heat of the midday sun in order to facilitate television coverage. It was 98 degrees on the pitch and the England players sweated to an average weight loss of 10 pounds. Despite that, Gordon Banks pulled off a fantastic save. The next time you see a rerun of it, note carefully that what makes the save even more incredible is the fact that Banks reacted so quickly that he was able to cock back his right wrist and 'bat' the ball, on its upward journey, after banging into the ground, in front of the line and upwards to safety. And all that after having to scamper across his

MOST OVERRATED ENGLAND PLAYER

BRIAN LABONE. By this time he had relegated Jack Charlton to position of reserve centre half in Ramsey's mind, though the Leeds' veteran was still more of a goal threat than the Everton stopper. Labone was found wanting in the crucial quarter-final when he was woefully out of position for the third and decisive German goal. A cross to the far post drew Labone out of the middle allowing Muller to hook home the goal that sank England.

goal from the opposite post. As Pelé thumped his header downwards, he supposedly had the word 'goal' out before the ball sailed over the bar.

Later in the game, Jeff Astle might have earned England a draw but missed from a position almost identical to that from which he had won West Brom the 1968 FA Cup. As it happened, even a draw would not have improved England's qualification chances, so a win over Czechoslovakia would have to suffice.

Ramsey recalled Keith Newton, Jack Charlton came back in place of Labone, Bell replaced Ball and Allan Clarke made his international debut (in place of Francis Lee), while Astle replaced Hurst.

After a poor game, decided by an Allan Clarke penalty, the weather conditions (too much bright sunshine) were offered as the excuse for England's poor passing. Their pale blue shirts were indistinguishable from Czechoslovakia's white shirts in the sunlight. Which is almost on a par with 'the dog ate my homework' as excuses go, but it didn't really matter, because England were in the quarter-finals and faced West Germany three days later.

THEY'RE COMING BACK HOME

Unfortunately, Gordon Banks either drank some dodgy beer or ate something that didn't agree with him— he once claimed that he must have 'contracted something

MOST DANGEROUS OPPONENT

PELÉ. Jairzinho may have scored the goal that beat England in the group game and Muller might have been the thorn in England's side, but Pelé (above with Bobby Moore) masterminded Brazil's march to winning the World Cup.

Pelé thought he'd scored – but Banks (on ground by left post) pushed the header up and over the bar. Bobby Moore (centre) looks relieved

from the side of his dinner plate' and with an hour's notice, Peter Bonetti was told he was playing. It wasn't the only thing to go wrong that day.

Sir Alf's wife had to watch the game from a TV back in her husband's hotel room as her seat in the stadium was occupied by a local who refused to budge. Amazingly, officials were unable to find the wife of the World Champions' team manager another seat!

As the teams lined up, nostalgists noted both sets of players were attired as they had been exactly four years earlier, the Germans in white and England in red. That was where the similarities ended.

Alan Mullery scored his first international goal to put England ahead after half an hour and Peters doubled the lead just four minutes into the second half.

Schoen, the German coach, then took the calculated gamble of replacing Libuda with a similarly direct winger, Grabowski. With Cooper apparently knackered after spending an hour subduing Libuda, Grabowski turned the game for the Germans.

While Ramsey was considering saving Bobby Charlton for the semi-final and sending Bell into the fray, Beckenbauer fired in a bobbly shot that crept under Bonetti to reduce the arrears, midway through the second period. Despite the goal, Ramsey made the change. But for all his athleticism, Bell was not Bobby. Beckenbauer, now free from the constraints of having to man-mark Charlton, began to exert an influence in what was his 106th game for his national team, and

MOST DANGEROUS ENGLAND PLAYER

GORDON BANKS was clearly the best goalkeeper in the world and proved it with the most memorable save in World Cup history, to deny Pelé. His value to the team was underlined when he was forced out of the quarter-final through illness. Would the errors in defence that led to England's exit have occurred with 'Banks of England' between the sticks?

Official programme all the way from Mexico, and only six shillings

WORLD CUP 1970 RESULTS

GROUP 3 WINNERS: BRAZIL (ENGLAND QUALIFIED)
England 2nd P3/W2/D0/L1/F2/A1
England 1 [Hurst] v Romania 0
2 June 1970 (Guadalajara)
Brazil 1 [Jairzinho] v England 0
7 June 1970 (Guadalajara)
England 1 [Clarke (pen)] v Czechoslovakia 0
11 June 1970 (Guadalajara)

QUARTER-FINAL
West Germany 3 [Beckenbauer, Seeler, Muller] v England 2 [Mullery, Peters]
14 June 1970 (Leon)

THE FINAL
Brazil 4 [Pelé, Gerson, Jairzinho, Carlos Alberto] v Italy 1 [Boninsegna]
21 June 1970 (Mexico City)

Germany equalised. Uwe Seeler, 34 and playing his 19th World Cup finals match, looped a header over a stranded Peter Bonetti in the English goal and the initiative was with the Germans.

Extra-time in sweltering heat didn't seem to bother Grabowski and he engineered the winner (after Hurst had a 'goal' disallowed). From the winger's cross the ball was headed back across goal. Bonetti was out of position again and Muller volleyed home to win the game. It was the second meeting between the teams since July 1966 and the Germans had won both.

The English team flew back home no longer World Champions, little knowing that England wouldn't get even as much as a sniff of even playing in a World Cup finals for twelve years.

And that bracelet was never found.

BRITISH HOME INTERNATIONAL CHAMPIONSHIPS 1967–70

The Home Internationals had been introduced in 1884 as a competition between the national British football teams, only. England won the first game in Belfast, 8-1. A century later they drew the last game in Glasgow 1-1. Which says it all, really...

HOME INTERNATIONAL CHAMPIONSHIPS 1966–67								
ENGLAND	P3	W2	D0	L1	F9	A4	GD4	PTS4
(Winners: Scotland)								
N. Ireland 0 v England 2 [Hurst, Charlton R]								
22 Oct 1966 (Belfast)								
England 5 [Hurst 2, Charlton R, Charlton J, Hennessey (o.g.)] v Wales 1 [Davies]								
16 Nov 1966 (Wembley)								
England 2 [Charlton J, Hurst] v Scotland 3 [Law, Lennox, McCalliog]								
15 April 1967 (Wembley)								

HOME INTERNATIONAL CHAMPIONSHIPS 1967–68								
ENGLAND	P3	W2	D1	L0	F6	A1	GD5	PTS5
(Winners: England)								
Wales 0 v England 3 [Peters, Charlton R, Ball (pen)]								
21 Oct 1967 (Cardiff)								
England 2 [Hurst, Charlton R] v N. Ireland 0								
22 Nov 1967 (Wembley)								
Scotland 1 [Hughes] v England 1 [Peters]								
24 Feb 1968 (Hampden Park)								

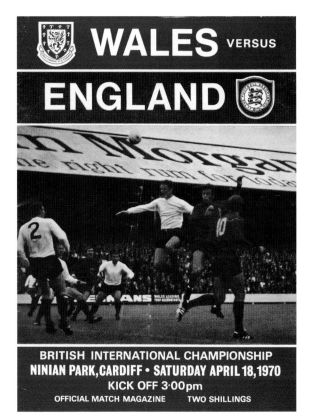

BRITISH INTERNATIONAL CHAMPIONSHIP
NINIAN PARK, CARDIFF • SATURDAY APRIL 18, 1970
KICK OFF 3·00pm
OFFICIAL MATCH MAGAZINE   TWO SHILLINGS

Wales managed a draw in Cardiff and shared the Championship in 1970

Sir Alf used only 25 players in the Home Internationals during this four-year period, eight of whom made it to Mexico for the 1970 World Cup (Jimmy Greaves found his own way there by taking part in the London–Mexico World Cup rally and finished sixth.)

The Home Internationals of 1967 and 1968 were used as qualifiers for the 1968 Euros and also introduced the game to a new rule: goalkeepers could take only four steps while holding the ball.

HOME INTERNATIONAL CHAMPIONSHIPS 1969

ENGLAND	P3	W3	D0	L0	F9	A3	GD6	PTS6

(Winners: England)

N. Ireland 1 [McMordie] v England 3 [Peters, Lee, Hurst (pen)]

3 May 1969 (Belfast)

England 2 [Charlton R, Lee] v Wales 1 [Davies]

7 May 1969 (Wembley)

England 4 [Peters (2), Hurst (2, I pen)] v Scotland 1 [Stein]

10 May 1969 (Wembley)

HOME INTERNATIONAL CHAMPIONSHIPS 1970

ENGLAND	P3	W1	D2	L0	F4	A2	GD2	PTS4

(Joint Winners: England, Scotland and Wales)

Wales 1 [Krzywicki] v England 1 [Lee]

18 April 1970 (Cardiff)

England 3 [Charlton R, Hurst, Peters] v N. Ireland 1 [Best]

21 April 1970 (Wembley)

Scotland 0 v England 0

25 April 1970 (Hampden Park)

COMBINED TABLE HOME INTERNATIONAL CHAMPIONSHIPS 1966–70

	P	W	D	L	F	A	GD	PTS(/24)
England	12	8	3	1	28	10	10	19
Scotland	12	5	5	2	19	16	3	15
Wales	12	2	5	5	12	19	-7	7
N. Ireland	12	1	3	8	5	17	-12	5

PLAYERS USED BY ENGLAND

MANAGER: SIR ALF RAMSEY

GOALKEEPERS	CLUB (MOVED TO/WHEN)
Gordon Banks	Stoke City
Peter Bonetti	Chelsea
DEFENDERS	
George Cohen	Fulham
Ray Wilson	Everton
Keith Newton	Blackburn (Everton/1969)
Bob McNab	Arsenal
Terry Cooper	Leeds
Bobby Moore	West Ham
Jack Charlton	Leeds
David Sadler	Man Utd
Brian Labone	Everton
Norman Hunter	Leeds
MIDFIELDERS	
Martin Peters	West Ham
Bobby Charlton	Man Utd
Nobby Stiles	Man Utd
Alan Ball	Everton
Alan Mullery	Tottenham
Peter Thompson	Liverpool
Mike Summerbee	Man City
Colin Bell	Man City
FORWARDS	
Roger Hunt	Liverpool
Geoff Hurst	West Ham
Jimmy Greaves	Tottenham
Francis Lee	Man City
Jeff Astle	West Brom

English league teams started to flourish in European competitions when Man Utd became the first English club to win the European Cup in 1968. Leeds, who had been losing finalists in the Fairs Cup in 1967, won it in 1968 and were followed a year later by Newcastle, whose Bryan 'Pop' Robson bought his wife a washing machine with his win bonus. Arsenal completed an English hat-trick in 1970.

Bobby Charlton (1966) and George Best (1968) were voted European Footballer of the Year in their respective years. Even the Scots succeeded in Europe: Celtic won the 1967 European Cup.

EUROPEAN CHAMPIONSHIPS BELGIUM 1972

'ENGLAND SCRAPE A WIN IN THE SUN'

(*EVENING STANDARD*)

After the disappointment of the 1970 World Cup, England expected their national team to regain some credibility in the world game at the European Championships of 1972. Sir Alf Ramsey was still in charge of the national team, but he knew he had to make changes and bring in new players because many of his heroes of 1966 had retired from international football – or been 'retired' by him, usually without even a letter of thanks to inform them. He still had the younger players of '66 to rely on of course, people like

ENGLAND SQUAD 1971 BACK L-R: Lee, Ball, Peters, Chivers, Mullery, Moore, Osgood, Banks, Lloyd, Reaney. FRONT L-R: Hurst, McNab, Storey, Hollins, McFarland, Coates, Hughes. They went on to beat Switzerland 3-2 in Basle

Ball, Hurst and Peters, while Gordon Banks was still the Number 1 goalkeeper and in the young Peter Shilton, he had a very able deputy. Yet Sir Alf was determined to create a new England from largely untested players, 'blooding' them in actual competition. At least to begin with.

For England's opening qualifying game against Malta in February 1971, Sir Alf brought Roy McFarland, Joe Royle, Martin Chivers and Colin Harvey into the team. Unfortunately England only just scrambled a 1-0 win that night (scorer Martin Peters).

For the next qualifying game, against Greece, Sir Alf gave Arsenal 'hard-man' Peter Storey a debut, while retaining only McFarland and Chivers – who scored his first England goal in a 3-0 win – from the first match, and also bringing in Ralph Coates for his second cap.

Chris Lawler, Liverpool's goalscoring full back, made his debut in the return game against Malta and promptly scored, as did Chivers again, twice. Francis Lee also netted, along with Allan Clarke, from a penalty, in only his second game for England. Remarkably, Malta won NO corners during the game, England had NO goal kicks and Gordon Banks' FOUR touches were all from back passes.

When the qualifying games resumed late in 1971 in Basle against Switzerland, Hurst, Chivers and an own goal from Weibel gave England another win (although Switzerland scored two in reply). Arsenal's John Radford and Leeds' Paul Madeley won their second caps that night, but Radford couldn't keep his place for the return at Wembley, where the Swiss forced a 1-1 draw, with Man City's Summerbee the English goalscorer (his first) and Peter Shilton in goal. Hurst and Chivers ensured the year ended on a positive note for England with victory in Greece, putting England at the top of their qualifying group.

They were through to the quarter-finals.

ENGLAND SQUAD				
	CLUB	AGE	CAPS	GOALS
GOALKEEPERS				
Gordon Banks	Stoke City	34	68	
Peter Shilton	Leicester	22	2	
FULL BACKS				
Paul Madeley	Leeds	28	3	
Paul Reaney	Leeds	27	2	
Chris Lawler	Liverpool	28	3	1
Terry Cooper	Leeds	28	17	
CENTRE BACKS				
Alan Mullery	Tottenham	30	34	1
Norman Hunter	Leeds	28	14	1
Roy McFarland	Derby	24	6	
Larry Lloyd	Liverpool	23	1	
Bobby Moore	West Ham	31	91	2
MIDFIELDERS				
Peter Storey	Arsenal	26	3	
Colin Bell	Man City	26	14	2
Emlyn Hughes	Liverpool	24	13	
Alan Ball	Everton	27	52	7
Martin Peters	Tottenham	28	50	18
Mike Summerbee	Man City	29	3	1
Colin Harvey	Everton	27	1	
FORWARDS				
John Radford	Arsenal	25	1	
Allan Clarke	Leeds	26	3	2
Francis Lee	Man City	28	25	9
Martin Chivers	Tottenham	27	7	6
Geoff Hurst	West Ham	30	47	23
Ralph Coates	Burnley	26	3	
Rodney Marsh	QPR	27	1	
Joe Royle	Everton	23	1	

'WEST GERMANS HAVE EYE ON EUROPEAN TITLE' (JACK ROLLIN)

Four months later the first leg, against West Germany, was played at Wembley. Despite England having lost to them in Mexico, there was no feeling of trepidation about the opposition. Indeed, the programme for that game on Saturday 29 April 1972 demonstrated the English superiority, by way of a listing of West Germany's full international record. It showed that in 14 games played against England (including amateur matches) the West Germans had won just 2, and lost 10.

For those watching in black and white that day, the Germans wore green shirts – which matched the English fans' faces as they witnessed a marvellous display from the Germans. With Gunter Netzer, a kind of German Bobby Charlton, showing great flair and athleticism, running the game in midfield, Ball, Bell and Peters couldn't get near him.

England were fortunate to only trail by an Uli Houness goal at the interval. Of course it got worse. There was something sadly symbolic about the withdrawal of Geoff Hurst, to be replaced by Rodney Marsh, for the second time in three internationals. The Man City star would only ever score one goal in nine games for England but he replaced a hero of just six years earlier. Against the same opposition, on the same pitch, Hurst trudged out of international football, just one cap short of the half century, having scored 24.

England equalised through Francis Lee, who became (at time of writing) the last England player to score on his birthday (his 28th) with 13 minutes to go. However, a draw would have been extremely lucky for England, and ill-deserved. It would have staved off progress for the Germans to the semi-finals in Belgium though, at least until after the return game in Berlin.

But the Germans couldn't wait that long, and Gunter Netzer capped a wonderful individual display by converting a penalty awarded after Banks had decked

Held. Their third goal, from 'Der Bomber' Gerd Muller, merely confirmed what many England fans already knew: the West Germans were much better than their team.

Needing to pull back two goals in the second leg, Ramsey decided to pair Marsh and Chivers up front (causing bafflement among fans, the press and apparently the players, too) and stiffen midfield with

EUROPEAN CHAMPIONSHIPS 1972 QUALIFYING

GROUP 3 WINNERS: ENGLAND

England P6/W5/D1/L0/F15/A3
Malta 0 v England 1 [Peters]
3 Feb 1971 (Valetta)
England [Chivers, Hurst, Lee] 3 v Greece 0
21 April 1971 (Wembley)
England 5 [Chivers (2), Lee, Clarke (pen), Lawler] v Malta 0
12 May 1971 (Wembley)
Switzerland 2 [Jeandupeux, Kunzli] v England 3 [Hurst, Chivers, Weibel (O.G.)]
13 October 1971 (Basle)
England [Summerbee] 1 v Switzerland 1 [Odermatt]
9 November 1971 (Wembley)
Greece 0 v England 2 [Hurst, Chivers]
1 December 1971 (Piraeus)

MOST DANGEROUS OPPONENT

GUNTER NETZER was a revelation when West Germany, in those awful green shirts, destroyed England at Wembley in April 1972. He was almost a typical English midfielder – only with the added qualities of touch, technique and athleticism. West Germany had Gunter, we had Ball, Peters and Bell. If only the Manchester City man had been as blessed as Netzer.

Hunter and Storey. It was hardly a line-up to inspire attacking optimism. But Storey did a job on Netzer, and without his orchestration West Germany didn't pose the threat they had at Wembley. England went out of the European Championships with an improved performance, but a goalless draw in Berlin. More than anything the two games against West Germany showed that they had progressed in their football development since 1966 and 1970, while England had not. The rest of the decade would prove exactly how much more progressive the Germans proved to be than the English.

The West Germans won the competition.

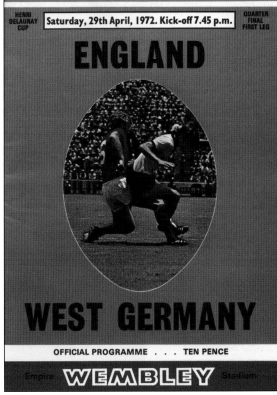

ABOVE: The original programme for the Wembley leg of the 1972 Euro Championships quarter-final

EUROPEAN CHAMPIONSHIPS 1972 RESULTS

QUARTER-FINAL 1ST LEG

England 1 [Lee] v West Germany 3 [Hoeness, Netzer, Muller]

29 April 1972 (Wembley)

Gordon Banks, Paul Madeley, Emlyn Hughes, Colin Bell, Bobby Moore, Norman Hunter, Francis Lee, Alan Ball, Martin Chivers, *Geoff Hurst, Martin Peters.

*Marsh, 61st min

QUARTER-FINAL 2ND LEG

West Germany 0 v England 0

13 May 1972 (Berlin)

Gordon Banks, Paul Madeley, Emlyn Hughes, Peter Storey, Roy McFarland, Bobby Moore, Alan Ball, Colin Bell, Martin Chivers, *Rodney Marsh, **Norman Hunter.

*Summerbee, 60th min, **Peters, 85th min

THE FINAL

West Germany [Muller 2, Wimmer] 3 v USSR 0

18 June 1972 (Brussels)

THE MANAGER: SIR ALF RAMSEY

After the qualified failure of Mexico '70 Ramsey's tactics were slated by the media. He steered England through the 1972 European Championships qualifiers easily enough, but failed when facing the West Germans again (in the quarter-final).

Sir Alf's influence was clearing slipping with the new generation of England players who were growing their hair long, acting more like George Best than Bobby Charlton and wanting to be individual stars, not just team players. England's manager didn't seem to know how to get the most from this new breed of player.

RAMSEY'S ENGLAND RECORD 14 JUNE 1970 – 13 MAY 1972						
P	W	D	L	F	A	WIN %
12	8	3	1	23	8	67

WORLD CUP WEST GERMANY 1974

WHO'S LAUGHING NOW, BRIAN?

Even though England got a lot closer to World Cup final matches in 1970 and 1990, there is something highly memorable about the failure to reach the 1974 finals in West Germany. The failure to beat Poland is a landmark in the last 40 years of trying to win something, and centres around that casual dismissal of a goalkeeper by Brian Clough, as a 'clown'.

The qualifying campaign began with Ramsey's 100th game in charge against Wales, but without Gordon Banks. He had lost an eye in a road crash which ended his career. That left only Bobby Moore and Alan Ball from the '66 team still playing for England.

Ramsey gave Liverpool teammates Ray Clemence and Kevin Keegan their debuts at Ninian Park where England struggled to win 1-0. The performance saw established players and newcomers failing to lift each other in a team which lacked a potent strike force or midfield creativity. The return at Wembley saw a Norman Hunter goal earn a point, after Toshack had fired Wales ahead. The first time England had dropped a home point in a World Cup qualifier, it was an ominous foretaste of what was to come against Poland.

When England went to Chorzow in the summer of

SIR ALF'S LAST ENGLAND SQUAD 1974 L-R BACK: Shepherdson, Peters, Storey, Dobson, Brooking, Watson, Stevenson, Parkes, MacDonald, Ramsey
FRONT L-R: Bowles, Channon, Todd, Nish, Pejic, Beattie. They went on to draw 0-0 in Lisbon with Portugal and a month later Sir Alf was sacked

1973 the fact that Wales had beaten Poland 2-0 meant a win for Ramsey would eliminate the Poles. Even a draw would have sufficed but what transpired helped toward England's elimination later that same year.

Whether it was the venue, set in the heart of the Silesian coalfields, or the poor performances that preceded it, there was universal pessimism for the game that was broadcast live in the early evening.

Ramsey selected Shilton and Allan Clarke in place of Clemence and Keegan. Madeley came in at right back, allowing Peter Storey to push into midfield.

The nature of the sloppy goal England conceded after seven minutes summed up the team at that time. Gadocha's free-kick cannoned off Moore, then Shilton and into the net, though the Poles credited Gadocha with the goal. England dominated the game after going behind and Peters, Chivers and Clarke all had chances to score, without doing so. The second half began in a similar fashion until a mistake by Bobby Moore, giving the ball away to Lubanski, the fastest player on the field, saw him fire a shot home, in off the post. England, losing the game, then lost the plot and angry exchanges between the benches followed the dismissal of Alan Ball for grabbing Cmikiewicz warmly by the throat and introducing his knee to the groin of the Pole.

HA HA SAID THE CLOWN

England fans of a certain age will vividly remember the return match on the night of 17 October 1973. Brian Clough's pronouncement on English television that Polish goalkeeper Tomaszewski was 'a clown' seemed to inspire the giant Pole (winning his 13th cap) to one of the greatest goalkeeping displays seen at Wembley.

Poland came into the game having beaten Wales, which meant that England had to beat the Poles. Ramsey dropped Moore (also dropped by his club at the time), and hoped Norman Hunter would nullify the attacking threat of Deyna, from midfield.

THE MANAGER: SIR ALF RAMSEY

After the failure to qualify for the last four of the 1972 European Championships, Sir Alf tried new players and rejected former stalwarts such as the Charlton brothers in attempting to reach the 1974 World Cup finals. But trying to fit young, emerging players into his playing system meant England failed to reach the finals in West Germany. Sir Alf was sacked in April 1974, although the decision wasn't made public for ten days while the FA sought a replacement. At the time Sir Alf's manner and style of management was blamed for the team's failure, and yet his successors in the job didn't fare much better, using much the same squad.

After managing Birmingham City in 1977–78, Sir Alf retired from the game. He suffered a stroke during the 1998 World Cup and died, possibly unable to remember that he'd won anything in his career, of Alzheimer's in 1999, aged 79.

In 1966 Ramsey took a group of good players and three world-class stars (Moore, Charlton R, Banks), and moulded them into world beaters. In doing so he had a more worrying and long-term effect on English football. His wariness of flamboyant, individual players and his success without them has had a residual effect on subsequent England managers. Players who put in the effort, work-rate and battling qualities like Nobby Stiles, Ray Wilson, Roger Hunt and Jack Charlton are considered 'honest' and to represent the so-called 'Bulldog Spirit' so valued by press and Sunday League football fans alike. In later years the likes of Stuart Pearson, Terry McDermott and Darren Anderton would be seen as more 'reliable' than players such as Stan Bowles (5 caps), Graham Rix (17 caps, 5 as sub) or Matt Le Tissier (8 caps, 5 as sub). Still, Sir Alf will always be remembered for winning the World Cup, which is more than can be said for any other England manager.

RAMSEY'S ENGLAND RECORD 20 MAY 1972 – 3 APRIL 1974

P	W	D	L	F	A	WIN %
18	9	5	4	28	9	50

'I... MESSED THINGS UP A LITTLE.'

(NORMAN HUNTER)

England set about Poland with a vengeance from the kick-off. Space precludes cataloguing the chances England created, but suffice it to say that the ball hit everything (defenders, the 'keeper, post, and bar) EXCEPT the net.

More than three decades later, the game still conjures up two indelible images, defining moments just seconds apart. At 0-0 a Polish clearance, upfield, was heading for the tunnel, around the halfway line. Norman Hunter moved to cut out the break as Poland's Lato chased the ball. Watching eyes expected the Pole to end up in intensive care, or the Royal Box at the very least, but he didn't. Everyone in football knows what happened next but no-one tells it better than old 'Bites

Yer Legs', as Norman is 'fondly' remembered.

'I don't think I played in a more one-sided game in my entire top-flight career,' begins the Leeds enforcer, continuing, 'I saw the break and moved towards the ball but messed things up a little. On reflection, the ball should have ended up on the North Circular Road but I slowed up and like an idiot, instead of putting my foot through the ball I tried to lift it with my right foot. I must have had a brain seizure because never before, or after, did I do that and the ball went past me. So did Lato.'

Lato fed the ball, through the legs of the retreating Emlyn Hughes, to Domarski, whose shot went close to Shilton, then doing a passable impersonation of collapsing scaffolding, to go under his body and Poland were ahead. Norman said in the aftermath of the recriminations, 'Although I missed the challenge

MOST DANGEROUS ENGLAND PLAYER

There wasn't one. With the plethora of goalscorers available, when it mattered, against Wales, at Wembley, and in both games against Poland, the two goals that were scored in open play came from a midfielder and a centre back.

MOST DANGEROUS OPPONENT

JAN TOMASZEWSKI. Ridiculed by Brian Clough as 'A Clown', the Polish 'keeper had the last laugh. Not only did he defy England twice (seen here saving from Allan Clarke), but he kept a clean sheet against Brazil in the third place play-off for the 1974 World Cup.

MOST OVERRATED ENGLAND PLAYER

PETER SHILTON followed Gordon Banks, and may have gone on to surpass a record of 125 England caps if he hadn't been continually swapped with Ray Clemence as England's 'keeper. However, of the three goals conceded by England against Poland, two were down to his error.

I still think Peter Shilton could have saved it. He could have thrown his cap on it to be honest.' Which roughly translates as, 'Not my fault guv'nor, the goalie should have stopped it.'

Despite Allan Clarke scoring a late penalty equaliser, the draw wasn't enough, England were out and Ramsey's days were numbered as manager of England. Tomaszewski went on to star as Poland finished third in the 1974 World Cup finals.

In a three-team, four-game group, England had won one, drawn two and lost one of their matches in yet another unsuccessful qualifying campaign. For several years Ramsey had exercised extreme caution in his team selection and played a strong defence. But when it became necessary for his sides to switch into attacking mode, they could not.

WORLD CUP 1974 QUALIFYING GAMES

GROUP 5 WINNERS POLAND

England 2nd P4/W1/D2/L1/F3/A4 did not qualify

Wales 0 v England 1 [Bell]

15 Nov 1972 (Cardiff)

Ray Clemence, Peter Storey, Emlyn Hughes, Norman Hunter, Roy McFarland, Bobby Moore, Kevin Keegan, Rodney Marsh, Martin Chivers, Colin Bell, Alan Ball.

England 1 [Hunter] v Wales 1 [Toshack]

24 Jan 1973 (Wembley)

Ray Clemence, Peter Storey, Emlyn Hughes, Norman Hunter, Roy McFarland, Bobby Moore, Kevin Keegan, Colin Bell, Martin Chivers, Rodney Marsh, Alan Ball.

Poland 2 [Moore (o.g.), Lubanski] v England 0

6 June 1973 (Chorzow)

Peter Shilton, Paul Madeley, Emlyn Hughes, Peter Storey, Roy McFarland, Bobby Moore, Alan Ball, Colin Bell, Martin Chivers, Allan Clarke, Martin Peters.

England 1 [Clarke (pen)] v Poland 1 [Domarski]

17 Oct 1973

Peter Shilton, Paul Madeley, Emlyn Hughes, Colin Bell, Roy McFarland, Norman Hunter, Tony Currie, Mick Channon, *Martin Chivers.

*Kevin Hector, 85th min

THE FINAL

Holland 1 [Neeskens] v West Germany 2 [Breitner, Muller]

7 July 1974 (Munich)

EUROPEAN CHAMPIONSHIPS YUGOSLAVIA 1976

'I'M THE BEST MAN FOR THE JOB' (DON REVIE)

After the dismal showing for the 1974 World Cup there was a lot riding on qualification for the 1976 European Championships and Don Revie, the successor to Sir Alf Ramsey as England manager, knew it. Ramsey had been sacked on 19 April 1974, two weeks after he'd seen his team held to a goalless draw in Portugal and a whole six months after he'd failed to qualify for the World Cup in Germany.

Revie claimed that he approached the FA for the vacant position after the news was made public on May 1 1974. The FA took a little over six weeks to make a deal with the Leeds Utd manager. They could have had Clough. They could have had Allison. They could have kept Joe Mercer (caretaker for a short while) or even Ron Greenwood. Instead they got Don Revie and his thick dossiers of data on every opponent that they were to face. He liked to know the stats, and liked his players and staff to know them too.

Revie had three months to prepare for the opening qualifier of the 1976 European Championships against

ENGLAND SQUAD 1976, AT LA AIRPORT L-R: Royle, Taylor W, Odell, Clemence, Gillard, McFarland, Francis G, Cherry, Wilkins, Todd, Millichip, Towers, Corrigan, Unknown, Stephen (Sir Andrew), Parkin, Greenhoff, Brooking, Pearson, Doyle, Hill, Taylor P, Mills, Clement, Medhurst, Rimmer, Keegan, Channon, Cocker, Neal, Swales, Street, Unknown, Revie. It was a big FA jolly to the Bicentennial Tournament. They didn't have anything else to do

EUROPEAN FOOTBALL CHAMPIONSHIP

HENRI
DELAUNAY
CUP

WEDNESDAY, 16th APRIL 1975

GROUP ONE
QUALIFYING
COMPETITION

ENGLAND v CYPRUS

Official
Programme
Fifteen pence

WEMBLEY
STADIUM

Kick
off
7.45 p.m.

The night that Malcolm 'Super Mac' MacDonald scored five goals at Wembley was also the last time he scored for England

Czechoslovakia, at Wembley. Clearly his dossiers were well prepared, because England won 3-0 (the Czechs then went on a run of 23 unbeaten games). Something went wrong in the next game a month later though, and England drew 0-0 against a Portuguese side that Czechoslovakia had scored five against. English supporters and the media were outraged, but Revie and the FA knew how to handle them – beat West Germany, the World Champions. So they did, 2-0 at Wembley in March 1975.

A month later Malcolm MacDonald became the first Englishman to score five goals for his country at Wembley, against Cyprus in their next qualifying game.

Denis Tueart made his debut and it was Ray Clemence's turn in goal (it would be Peter Shilton next), when England won 1-0 in the return game in Limassol, with a Keegan goal.

Six wins and three draws in his first nine games should have been cause for England optimism but according to the media, Revie was finding it hard to keep his international players happy.

'WHOSE TURN IS IT, DON?'

In 1975 Don Revie employed a revolutionary rotation policy for England players. The only problem was, no-one knew what that meant. The players didn't appear to

THE MANAGER: DON REVIE

Revie's first game with England went well enough and he started as he meant to go on – by making changes. There were debuts for QPR pair Dave Thomas and Gerry Francis and England beat Czechoslovakia 3-0 in a European Championships qualifier but then failed to impress in drawing 0-0 against Portugal in the next (friendly) game.

Revie liked to 'manage' in the manner of Sir Alf Ramsey, telling his players only what he thought they needed to know. In March 1975 he replaced Emlyn Hughes, a born leader, with Alan Ball, who always walked a disciplinary tightrope, as England captain. He capped Alan Hudson twice before dropping him and never picking the striker again.

In 1976 Alan Ball's wife was contacted by a journalist asking for her comment about her husband being replaced as England skipper by Gerry Francis. Her husband didn't learn officially until the next day and then it was through Revie's office and not from his manager.

REVIE'S ENGLAND RECORD 30TH OCT 1974 – 19 NO, 1975						
P	W	D	L	F	A	WIN %
11	6	4	1	22	7	54.5%

know what Revie was doing, and even he often seemed unsure. In his first eight games he used 27 different players, with Dave Watson the only ever-present. He would drop players, without warning, Alan Hudson being the prime example. Hudson, who Ramsey stated should have been taken to Mexico as an untried teenager, was given his first cap by Revie, and was a revelation against West Germany in that 2-0 friendly victory. But he won his second and final cap against Cyprus the following month!

Revie's selection policy was crucified when the real business of European Championships qualification resumed after the Home Internationals and a 2-1 friendly victory over Switzerland. Of the starting line-up that faced the Swiss, only five started in Bratislava against the Czechs, in October 1975.

MOST DANGEROUS ENGLAND PLAYER

MICK CHANNON was not a blustering centre forward like Malcolm MacDonald or a 'sniffer' of goals like Allan Clarke, but he did combine strength and subtlety, as well as having an eye for goal. He scored three goals in six qualifiers plus another three in four friendlies, against Argentina (above), East Germany and Yugoslavia during the same period.

MOST OVERRATED ENGLAND PLAYER

KEVIN KEEGAN played in the last four qualifiers and scored once. He couldn't even get in on the act when Cyprus were crushed at Wembley, although he did score the only goal in the away game. When goals were needed against Portugal and Czechoslovakia he was found wanting.

EUROPEAN CHAMPIONSHIPS 1976 QUALIFYING

GROUP 1 WINNERS: CZECHOSLOVAKIA

England 2nd P6/W3/D2/L1/F11/A3 (did not qualify)

England 3 [Colin Bell (2), Mick Channon] v Czechoslovakia 0

30 Oct 1974 (Wembley)

Ray Clemence, Paul Madeley, Emlyn Hughes, *Martin Dobson, Dave Watson, Norman Hunter, Colin Bell, Gerry Francis, **Frank Worthington, Mick Channon, Kevin Keegan.

*Trevor Brooking, 64th min **Dave Thomas, 64th min

England 0 v 0 Portugal

20 Nov 1974 (Wembley)

Ray Clemence, Paul Madeley, *Terry Cooper, Emlyn Hughes, Dave Watson, Trevor Brooking, Colin Bell, Gerry Francis, Mick Channon, **Allan Clarke, Dave Thomas.

 *Colin Todd, 23rd min **Frank Worthington, 70th min

England 5 [Macdonald (5)] v Cyprus 0

16 April 1975 (Wembley)

Peter Shilton, Paul Madeley, Kevin Beattie, Colin Todd, Dave Watson, Colin Bell, Alan Ball, Malcolm MacDonald, *Mick Channon, Alan Hudson, Kevin Keegan.

 *Dave Thomas, 65th min

Cyprus 0 v England 1 [Keegan]

11 May 1975 (Limassol)

Ray Clemence, Steve Whitworth, *Kevin Beattie, Colin Todd, Dave Watson, Colin Bell, **Dave Thomas, Malcolm MacDonald, Mick Channon, Alan Ball, Kevin Keegan.

*Emlyn Hughes, 43rd min **Dennis Tueart, 73rd min

Czechoslovakia 2 [Nehoda, Gallis] v England 1 [Channon]

30 Oct 1975 (Bratislava)

Ray Clemence, Paul Madeley, Ian Gillard, Gerry Francis, *Roy McFarland, Colin Todd, Kevin Keegan, **Mick Channon, Malcolm MacDonald, Allan Clarke, Colin Bell.

 *Dave Watson, 46th min **Dave Thomas, 76th min

Portugal 1 [Rodrigues] v 1 England [Channon]

19 Nov 1975 (Lisbon)

Ray Clemence, Steve Whitworth, Kevin Beattie, Gerry Francis, Dave Watson, Colin Todd, Kevin Keegan, Mick Channon, *Malcolm MacDonald, Trevor Brooking, **Paul Madeley.

*Dave Thomas, 70th min **Allan Clarke, 70th min

THE FINAL

Czechoslovakia 2 [Svehlik, Dobias] v West Germany 2 [Muller, Holzenbein] AET (2-2)

Czechoslovakia 5-3 West Germany penalty shoot-out

20 Jun 1976 (Belgrade)

After the game had to be abandoned through fog, the rearranged fixture 24 hours later saw Mick Channon fire England ahead but Czechoslovakia hit back to win 2-1. If there was a defining result in the failed campaign, this was it, as it meant only a comprehensive win against Portugal in Lisbon on 19 November would qualify England for the finals.

Since beating them in the World Cup of 1966, England had played Portugal three times. The first game, a friendly, ended 1-0 to England at Wembley. The second, also a friendly, was Ramsey's last game in charge. Revie had overseen the 0-0 draw at Wembley in 1974. So what were the chances of a comprehensive English victory? The game ended in a 1-1 draw and the Czechs qualified, going on to win the Championships.

BRITISH HOME INTERNATIONAL CHAMPIONSHIPS 1971–75

HOME INTERNATIONAL CHAMPIONSHIPS 1971							
ENGLAND	P3	W2	D1	L0	F4	A1	GD3 PTS5
(Winners: England)							
N. Ireland 0 v England 1 [Clarke]							
15 May 1971 (Belfast)							
England 0 v Wales 0							
19 May 1971 (Wembley)							
England 3 [Chivers (2), Peters] v Scotland 1 [Curran]							
22 May 1971 (Wembley)							

HOME INTERNATIONAL CHAMPIONSHIPS 1973							
ENGLAND	P3	W3	D0	L0	F6	A1	GD5 PTS6
(Joint Winners: England and Scotland)							
N. Ireland 1 [Clements] v England 2 [Chivers 2]							
12 May 1973 (Goodison Park)							
England 3 [Chivers, Channon, Peters] v Wales 0							
15 May 1973 (Wembley)							
England [Peters] 1 v Scotland 0							
19 May 1973 (Wembley)							

HOME INTERNATIONAL CHAMPIONSHIPS 1972							
ENGLAND	P3	W2	D0	L1	F4	A1	GD3 PTS4
(Joint Winners: England and Scotland)							
Wales 0 v England 3 [Hughes, Marsh, Bell]							
20 May 1972 (Ninian Park)							
England 0 v N. Ireland 1 [Neill]							
23 May 1972 (Wembley)							
Scotland 0 v England 1 [Ball]							
27 May 1972 (Hampden)							

HOME INTERNATIONAL CHAMPIONSHIPS 1974							
ENGLAND	P3	W2	D0	L1	F3	A2	GD1 PTS4
(Joint Winners: England and Scotland)							
Wales 0 v England 2 [Bowles, Keegan]							
11 May 1974 (Ninian Park)							
England 1 [Weller] v N. Ireland 0							
15 May 1974 (Wembley)							
Scotland 2 [Jordan, Todd (o.g.)] v England 0							
18 May 1974 (Hampden)							

England used a total of 44 players in 15 British Championships games between 15 May 1971 and 24 May 1975, and three managers. Sir Alf Ramsey began the series using it as a proving ground to find players to take England to the World Cup of 1974, or before that, the European Championships 1972. He failed both times.

In 1974 he was sacked, just before the Home Internationals in May. One World Cup in 10 years was not enough, clearly, and the FA turned to one of the managers that the press had been suggesting for a while, Joe Mercer. He took the job only temporarily, however, and when at the end of the season a new man offered his services to the FA, they gratefully accepted. Don Revie was one of the most successful English managers at work in the game at the time. He may not have created a team that everyone – even staunch Leeds fans – loved, but they did win things.

CLOUGH FOR MANAGER!

As the dissatisfaction with Ramsey had grown, the media had led a campaign for Brian Clough to be made England manager. At Derby County, using players he had picked up from the lower leagues, he had made them League Champions and even European Cup

HOME INTERNATIONAL CHAMPIONSHIPS 1975

ENGLAND	P3	W1	D2	L0	F7	A3	GD4	PTS4
(Winners: England)								
N. Ireland 0 v England 0								
17 May 1975 (Belfast)								
England 2 [Johnson (2)] v Wales 2 [Toshack, Griffin]								
21 May 1975 (Wembley)								
England 5 [Francis T (2), Beattie, Bell, Johnson] v Scotland 1 [Rioch pen]								
24 May 1975 (Wembley)								

COMBINED TABLE HOME INTERNATIONAL CHAMPIONSHIPS 1971–75

	P	W	D	L	F	A	GD	PTS(/30)
England	15	9	3	3	22	8	14	21
Scotland	15	7	2	6	17	14	3	16
N. Ireland	15	6	3	6	6	10	-4	15
Wales	15	1	6	8	5	18	-13	8

contenders. But Old Big 'Ead's criticism of Ramsey and the FA did not help him get the job. As everyone knows, Clough was too outspoken for his own good. Cloughie could and did boast about his powers, his influence and his success. He also refused to use diplomacy in his dealings with those who ran football. The gentlemen of the FA who had power of decision over the national team could never appoint a self-made man of Clough's rough cut. How could they replace a knight of the realm who used received pronunciation with a commoner who flattened his 'a's? Which is why they went first for Mercer and then Revie, a man with all the charm (and the sheepskin coat) of a Conservative councillor.

For the first time, in 1971 the games were played over the space of a week at the end of the season. The first game of that series is best remembered for an audacious George Best 'goal', which was unfairly

PLAYERS USED BY ENGLAND

MANAGERS: SIR ALF RAMSEY (1971–73), JOE MERCER (1974), DON REVIE (1975)

GOALKEEPERS

Gordon Banks (Stoke City), Peter Shilton (Leicester City), Ray Clemence (Liverpool)

DEFENDERS

Steve Whitworth (Leicester City), Paul Madeley (Leeds), Peter Storey (Arsenal), Chris Lawler (Liverpool), Terry Cooper (Leeds), Bobby Moore (West Ham), Tommy Smith (Liverpool), David Nish (Derby County), Mike Pejic (Stoke City), Norman Hunter (Leeds), Ian Gillard (QPR), Roy McFarland (Derby County),Colin Todd (Derby County), Larry Lloyd (Liverpool)

MIDFIELDERS

Martin Peters (Tottenham), Dave Watson (Sunderland), Tony Currie (Sheff Utd), Alan Ball (Everton), Ralph Coates (Tottenham), Keith Weller (Liverpool), Mike Summerbee (Man City), Colin Bell (Man City), Colin Viljoen (Ipswich), Gerry Francis (QPR)

FORWARDS

David Johnson (Ipswich), Geoff Hurst (West Ham), Brian Little (Aston Villa), Francis Lee (Man City), Rodney Marsh (QPR, Man City 1972), Dennis Tueart (Man City), Martin Chivers (Tottenham), Allan Clarke (Leeds), Ally Brown (WBA), Malcolm MacDonald (Newcastle), Mick Channon (S'hampton), John Richards (Wolves), Kevin Keegan (Liverpool) Dave Thomas (QPR), Stan Bowles (QPR) Frank Worthington (Leicester)

disallowed. Best came from behind Banks as he went to clear his penalty area, headed the ball out of the goalkeeper's open palm, and rolled it into the net. The rules stated that the goalkeeper had to have both hands on the ball and Banks had just one, but the ref said it was 'ungentlemanly conduct' and so disallowed it.

WORLD CUP ARGENTINA 1978

IT TOOK TWO NOT TO TANGO

Failure to reach the 1974 World Cup finals meant that for the first time ever England were not seeded when it came to the qualifiers for Argentina '78. Luxembourg and Finland were (supposedly) the cannon fodder in the qualifying group but with only the top team going to South America, England had to eliminate perhaps the best team in Europe at the time. Italy had not failed to reach the finals for 20 years.

The opening game in Helsinki, in June 1976, was another opportunity for Revie to tinker with his selection, and significantly the last links with 1966 went with the omission of Alan Ball and Martin Peters from the team. Leeds pair Paul Madeley and Trevor Cherry replaced McFarland and Ray Kennedy while Stuart Pearson came in for Peter Taylor. Keegan, twice, Channon and Pearson scored the goals in a comfortable 4-1 win over Finland.

For the first time the FA postponed the First Division programme ahead of the return match, and England thanked them by doing the double over the Finns with two of Revie's five changes from the previous international, Joe Royle and Dennis Tueart, scoring in a 2-1 win at Wembley, in October.

Two England regulars, Mick Channon (left) and Colin Bell (far right), try another sport, along with sailor Chay Blyth and boxer John Strachey

'A HOLLOW, TAWDRY VICTORY' (*DAILY MIRROR*)

Revie's men might have beaten the Finns, but the inability to improve goal difference against a team of part-timers was to prove crucial and everyone except the manager seemed to know it. *The Times* called it 'a laborious, ineffective and insulting' win. Not for the first time since 1966, a technically superior set of players embarrassed England. And they were amateurs.

As Revie celebrated his second anniversary in charge he had to delay team selection for the vital game in Italy in November 1976, due to an epidemic of sore throats and colds which hit the squad.

That wasn't all to hit the line-up. Revie chose a completely new back line and a combative midfield designed to win the ball. But Trevor Brooking was the only player to do anything with the ball when won, and there was a lone front-runner in Stan Bowles (yes, I had to check it was him), so leaving out his previous two goalscorers Joe Royle and Stuart Pearson.

Italy had a formidable home record of only two defeats in 15 years. So Revie included a few choice Italian profanities in the dossiers he'd prepared for his team, to get them going. England managed to stifle Italy for half an hour but then the home side took a fortuitous lead when Antognoni's free kick was deflected past Clemence by Keegan.

Bettega's spectacular diving header with less than 15 minutes remaining confirmed victory. So, midway through the qualifying campaign, World Cup elimination loomed for England.

Luxembourg, like San Marino, is a nation more noted for its philatelic exports than its footballers and so when England faced the Duchy's finest, in the spring of 1977, hopes were high for a goal fest. All England had to do was run in a bucketful of goals in the two games before beating Italy, the former more achievable than the latter, maybe. Finland had already scored seven against Luxembourg, after all.

THE MANAGER: DON REVIE

Before the 1978 World Cup qualification began Revie refused to reveal his first team. He awarded 11 new caps in two consecutive games at the start of 1976. Of that number just Phil Neal and Mick Mills went on to develop meaningful international careers. While England were preparing in South America for a triple-header against Argentina, Brazil and Uruguay, Revie secretly met a United Arab Emirates delegation in Helsinki to discuss his managing the UAE team. The Football Association, blissfully unaware at the time, approached Revie about renewing his contract. Revie claimed he sought new employment because he thought the FA were about to sack him. In December 1978 an FA commission banned Revie from any involvement with English football for 10 years. A year on Revie had the ban overturned, but never worked in England again.

REVIE'S ENGLAND RECORD MARCH 1976 – JULY 1977

P	W	D	L	F	A	WIN %
19	8	5	6	27	18	42.1

THE MANAGER: RON GREENWOOD (1977)

After the sour experience of seeing the traitorous Revie desert the English World Cup '78 campaign in mid-sink, the FA reached out to Ron Greenwood. While in charge of West Ham Greenwood had nurtured the talents of the players who formed a large part of England's 1966 World Cup winning side – Moore, Hurst and Peters (he also took Jimmy Greaves to Upton Park after the tournament). It was hoped that his ability to develop young players combined with the respect given him by the older professionals in the squad would help create a miracle akin to that of the Hammers winning the FA Cup followed by the European Cup Winners Cup in 1964 and 1965. Unfortunately for everyone involved, Revie's legacy of confusion, distrust and bad results left Greenwood and England merely blowing bubbles back at home, watching the finals play out in Argentina on the telly.

England, decimated by injuries that robbed Revie of 10 players, gave a second cap to Trevor Francis, who scored two goals as did Mick Channon, with Ray Kennedy adding the other in a 5-0 win. In the seven months that passed before England went to Luxembourg for the return match, Don Revie skulked away to the United Arab Emirates, topping up his bank balance and tan but destroying his reputation. And so England appointed a new manager – Ron Greenwood. In June England's chances became decidedly dodgier after Italy beat Finland 3-0 and England had to score more than 5 in Luxembourg.

In only his second England game, and with goals the order of the day, the new England boss elected to play Emlyn Hughes as a sweeper, and give Ian Callaghan only his fourth (and final) cap 12 years after winning his first. England only managed to score twice, though, which meant that even if England beat Italy, the Italians would qualify as long as they beat Luxembourg. However, if England won by three goals at Wembley, the Azurri would need a three-goal winning margin against the Duchy.

Ron Greenwood selected three new caps to face Italy in November 1977, all attackers. Peter Barnes and Steve Coppell would provide the ammunition for Everton centre forward Bob Latchford. Trevor Francis

MOST DANGEROUS ENGLAND PLAYER

KEVIN KEEGAN. A busy, hardworking forward, who made up for a lack of natural ability with tremendous hard work. He scored four goals in the six World Cup qualifiers in which he played. Strangely, he only ever played for 26 minutes in one game in World Cup finals, in 1982.

MOST OVERRATED ENGLAND PLAYER

DON REVIE. Failure to reproduce club form on the international scene is not only a problem for players. Revie was the most successful club manager of his era, but in trying to replicate his methods on the international stage he failed miserably. Running away to the Middle East in the midst of trying to qualify cannot have been good for morale either.

was left on the bench. Keegan scored with a deflected header after just 10 minutes but there was never any danger of a goal torrent, although Barnes might have scored twice after England's opener.

To England's credit they turned on the style (so why not earlier in the campaign?), but a second goal didn't come until the 81st minute, through Brooking, and it wasn't enough. Italy duly beat Luxembourg 3-0, and England were eliminated on goal difference, the only nation to suffer that fate for that competition. Between them, Revie and Greenwood used 33 players in the six games, with only Clemence the ever-present.

When Revie left, only the Scots mourned: they'd beaten his side twice in a year, home and away.

THE 1978 WORLD CUP FINAL

Argentina 3 [Kempes (2), Bertoni] v Holland 1 [Naninga]
AET (1-1)
25 June 1978 (Buenos Aires)

WORLD CUP 1978 QUALIFYING

GROUP 2 WINNERS: ITALY

England 2nd P6/W5/D0/L1/F15/A4 did not qualify

Finland 1 [Paatelainen] v England 4 [Keegan (2), Channon, Pearson]
13 June 1976 (Helsinki)
Clemence, Todd, Mills, Thompson, Madeley, Cherry, Keegan, Channon, Pearson, Brooking, Francis G.

England 2 [Tueart, Royle] v Finland 1 [Nieminen]
13 Oct 1976 (Wembley)
Clemence, Todd, Beattie, Thompson, Greenhoff B, Wilkins, Keegan, Channon, Royle, *Brooking, **Tueart.
*Mills 75th min **Hill 75th min

Italy 2 [Antognoni, Bettega] v England 0
17 Nov 1976 (Rome)
Clemence, *Clement, Mills, Greenhoff, McFarland, Hughes, Keegan, Cherry, Channon, Bowles, Brooking.
*Beattie 75th min

England 5 [Channon (2, 1 pen) Kennedy, Francis T, Keegan] v Luxembourg 0
30 March 1977 (Wembley)
Clemence, Gidman, Cherry, Kennedy, Watson, Hughes, Keegan, Channon, *Royle, Francis T, Hill.
*Mariner 45th min

Luxembourg 0 v England 2 [Kennedy, Mariner]
12 October 1977 (Luxembourg City)
Clemence, Cherry, Hughes, *McDermott, **Watson, Kennedy, Wilkins, Francis T, Mariner, Hill, Callaghan.
*Whymark 65th min **Beattie 69th min

England 2 [Keegan, Brooking] v Italy 0
17 November 1977 (Wembley)
Clemence, Neal, Cherry, Wilkins, Watson, Hughes, *Keegan, Coppell, **Latchford, Brooking, Barnes P.
*Francis T 83rd min, **Pearson 75th min

ONE CAP WONDERS

Apart from Trevor Whymark, all of these players won medals and trophies during their club career, which is why they're my One Cap Wonders. None of them were picked by Sven, who tried to give every English player in the Premiership a cap during his time as England manager. They all (except Sutton and sub Marwood) got more minutes in an England shirt than Kevin Hector though, who wore it for 21 minutes over two games in 1973.

JOHN GIDMAN

(90 MINS, v LUXEMBURG 30/3/77, A WC QUALIFIER WIN 5-0)

Aston Villa ('71–'79), Everton ('79–'81), Man United ('81–'86), Manchester City ('86–'88), Stoke City ('88), Darlington ('88).

An overlapping right back with an eye for goal, played 433 games (19 goals), in a 17-year career. Won the FA Cup with Man Utd. Picked by Don Revie.

TOMMY SMITH

(90 MINS, v WALES 19/5/71, HOME INT 0-0)

Liverpool ('62–'78), Swansea ('78–'79)

Centre back. Played 637 games for Liverpool (48 goals). Won five League Championships, two FA Cups and the UEFA Cups, twice at Anfield. Scored twice in 36 league games for Swansea before retiring. Picked by Alf Ramsey.

DANNY WALLACE

(90 MINS, v EGYPT 29/1/86, FRIENDLY WIN 0-4, 1 GOAL)

Saints ('80–'89), Man Utd ('89–'93) Birmingham ('93–'95)

Not many players score on a debut and do not play again for England. Scored 79 goals in 317 games for Saints, won the FA and European Cup Winners' Cups with Man Utd. Diagnosed with MS in 1996 and retired. Picked by Bobby Robson.

JOHN HOLLINS

(90 MINS, v SPAIN 24/5/67, FRIENDLY WIN 2-0)

Chelsea ('63–'75, '83–'84), QPR ('75–'79), Arsenal ('79–'83)

A hard-tackling midfielder, retired in 1984 after 939 senior games. Won the FA Cup, the Football League Cup and the European Cup Winners' Cup as well as being a runner-up in each at Arsenal. Picked by Alf Ramsey.

SUBS

GK Nigel Spink (45 mins, v Australia 19/6/83, Friendly 1-1)

Tony Brown (72 mins, v Wales 19/5/71, Home Int 0-0)

Neil Ruddock (90 mins, v Nigeria 16/11/94, Friendly win 1-0)

Mark Walters (70 mins, v New Zealand 3/6/91, Friendly win 1-0)

Brian Marwood (10 mins, v Saudi Arabia 16/11/88, Friendly 1-1)

CHARLIE GEORGE

(65 MINS, v REP. IRELAND 8/9/76, FRIENDLY 1-1)

Arsenal ('68–'75), Derby County ('75–'78, '82), Saints ('78–'81), Bulova HK ('81–'82), Bournemouth ('82) Dundee Utd ('82–'83)

Picked for England five years after scoring the goal that won Arsenal the Double and a year after a hat-trick against Real Madrid for Derby. Substituted. Picked by Don Revie.

GK: JIMMY RIMMER
(PLAYED FIRST 45 MINS, v ITALY 28/5/76, FRIENDLY WIN 3-2)
Man United ('65–'74), Swansea ('73 on loan), (Arsenal '74–'77), Aston Villa ('77–'83), Swansea ('83–'86)

Won two European Cup winners' medals, with Man Utd in 1968 as a sub, and after playing only eight minutes for Aston Villa in 1982 (due to a neck injury). Picked by Don Revie.

DAVID UNSWORTH
(90 MINS, v JAPAN 3/6/95, UNBRO INT TOURNAMENT WIN 3-1)
Everton ('91–'97, '98–'04), West Ham ('97–'98), Villa ('98), Portsm'th ('04–'05), Sheff Utd ('05–'07), Wigan ('07–)

A tough centre back with a long career in the Premiership. 116 league games in first Everton spell, 188 in second. Still in the Premiership at time of writing. Picked by Terry Venables.

NICHOLAS PICKERING
(90 MINS, v AUSTRALIA 19/6/83, FRIENDLY 1-1)
Sunderland ('81–'86), Coventry ('86–'87) Derby County ('88–'91), Darlington ('91–'92), Burnley ('93)

Left back. Scored 18 goals in 209 games for Sunderland, nine in 78 for Coventry (also won the FA Cup), three in 45 for Derby, seven in 57 for Darlington. Picked by Bobby Robson.

COLIN HARVEY
(90 MINS, v MALTA 3/2/71, WC QUALIFIER WIN 0-1)
Everton ('63–'75), Sheff Wednesday ('74–'76)

Scored 24 goals in 384 games from midfield for Everton, two in 48 for Wednesday. Won the FA Cup in 1966 and 1970 First Division Championship with Everton, playing alongside Alan Ball and Howard Kendall. Picked by Alf Ramsey.

TREVOR WHYMARK
(25 MINS, v LUXEMBURG 12/10/77, WC QUALIFIER WIN 0-2)
Ipswich ('69–'79), Derby County ('79), Grimsby ('80–'84), Southend ('84–'85), Peterborough ('85), Colchester ('85)

Scored 75 goals for Ipswich in 261 games, including four years in the UEFA Cup. Came on as a sub for Terry McDermott with England leading only 1-0. Picked by Ron Greenwood.

CHRIS SUTTON
(11 MINS, v CAMEROON 15/11/97, FRIENDLY WIN 2-0)
Norwich ('91–'94), Blackburn Rovers ('94–'99), Chelsea ('99–'00), Celtic ('00–'06), Birmingham City ('06), Aston Villa ('06–)

Won a Premiership with Blackburn, 3 SPL titles, the FSA and League Cups twice at Celtic. Cost £21 million in transfer fees. Refused an England B squad call-up. Picked by Glenn Hoddle.

MANAGER: PETER TAYLOR
(90 MINS, v ITALY 15/11/00, FRIENDLY, LOST 1-0)

The only manager to take charge of England for one game, he put 16 players on the pitch in Turin and made David Beckham captain for the first time. Managed England Under 21 side twice, from 1996–'99 and 2004–'07, getting them to the European Championships finals in June 2007. Managed Leicester City in the Premiership 2000–'01. They were relegated, he was sacked. Manager Crystal Palace 2006– .

EUROPEAN CHAMPIONSHIPS ITALY 1980

WE'LL FIGHT THEM ON THE TERRACES

After the disappointment that was Don Revie, England enjoyed the thrill that was Ron Greenwood as manager. For the first time the European Championships saw eight teams qualify for the finals instead of the four of previous tournaments. Thus England's chances of getting to the finals were doubled, and they duly, almost spectacularly, took their chance. England qualified impressively, winning seven of their eight games and drawing the other, against the Republic of Ireland (the other teams were N. Ireland, Bulgaria and Denmark). England scored 22 goals and only let in five while qualifying and finished top of their group, six points ahead of second-placed N. Ireland.

The fans and the media were sure that, at last, England could win a proper trophy, only 14 years after the last.

All of which made their failure in Italy, where they finished third in their four-nation group, more baffling. The 'fans' didn't help much, resorting to the by now typical pasttime of indulging in alcohol-fuelled fighting with everyone and anyone who'd fight them.

The team began well enough in Italy with Ray Wilkins, not known for his pace or goalscoring, demonstrating both as he beat the Belgian off-side trap to score after half an hour of the Group B opener against Belgium. But a Ceulemans equaliser inside six

An England manager comforting tearful English players in Italy. Part 1: Ron Greenwood talks tactics with Keegan (7), Coppell and Brooking

ENGLAND SQUAD

	CLUB	AGE	CAPS	GOALS
GOALKEEPERS				
Ray Clemence	Liverpool	31	49	
Peter Shilton	Notts Forest	30	30	
Joe Corrigan	Man City	31	5	
FULL BACKS				
Phil Neal	Liverpool	29	25	3
Kenny Sansom	C Palace	21	7	
Viv Anderson	Notts Forest	23	3	
Trevor Cherry	Leeds	32	26	
Mick Mills	Ipswich Town	31	29	
CENTRE BACKS				
Dave Watson	S'hampton	33	49	4
Phil Thompson	Liverpool	26	23	1
Emlyn Hughes	Wolves	32	62	1
MIDFIELD				
Ray Wilkins	Man Utd	23	32	
Trevor Brooking	West Ham	31	37	2
Terry McDermott	Liverpool	28	10	
Ray Kennedy	Liverpool	28	15	3
Glenn Hoddle	Tottenham	22	3	2
FORWARDS				
Kevin Keegan	SV Hamburg	29	51	18
Steve Coppell	Man Utd	24	23	6
David Johnson	Liverpool	28	7	6
Tony Woodcock	FC Cologne	24	10	3
Paul Mariner	Ipswich Town	27	9	3
Garry Birtles	Notts Forest	23	1	

Previous page: BACK L-R: Anderson, Birtles, Barnes, Kennedy, Watson, Lloyd, Hoddle. MIDDLE L-R: Armstrong, Reeves, Neal, Shilton, Corrigan, Clemence, Thompson, Mariner, Johnson, Mills. FRONT L-R: Sansom, Cherry, McDermott, Hughes, Keegan, Woodcock, Wilkins, Coppell

THE MANAGER: RON GREENWOOD

Don Revie's legacy meant no 1978 World Cup for England but Ron had three matches, including the meaningless final qualifying games for that competition, to get used to the job before attempting to reach the 1980 European Championships. He didn't do too badly, to begin with. England began 1978 with two of the toughest friendlies imaginable and lost to West Germany before drawing with Brazil. Ron boosted confidence among his players, and England went into the Euro 1980 qualifiers on the back of four successive wins. The team breezed through the qualifying campaign but then failed to get beyond the group stages in Italy, in one of the worst showings by the national team in any competition. Still, he kept the job and aimed to qualify for the 1982 World Cup in Spain, which was up next.

GREENWOOD'S ENGLAND RECORD 7 SEPT 1977 – 18 JUNE 1980

P	W	D	L	F	A	WIN %
32	21	7	4	60	25	65.6

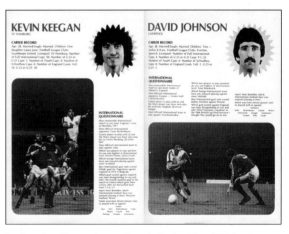

Profiles of two Liverpool greats from the England Euro 1980 brochure. Keegan's hair was not that spiky in real life

GARRY BIRTLES. Raw and young with only one cap. As he was to prove when he went to Manchester United, he was hardly a prolific goalscorer. And he had a beard. His playing style was too similar to Woodcock's and the pair never worked well together because they kept getting in each other's way.

BOB LATCHFORD scored 65 goals in 123 games for Everton in the three seasons leading up to the 1980 Euros. He had a better scoring record than Birtles, and was a more experienced player with 12 caps and five goals. His omission from the squad seems no less odd now than it did then.

minutes provoked fighting on the terraces and when the Italian police used tear gas to break it up, the spray covered the pitch and held up play. When the game resumed, players, with eyes streaming, struggled to breathe. Tony Woodcock's late 'goal' was ruled off-side, nearly a hundred fans were taken to hospital and the next day the Football Association was fined £8,000 by UEFA for their failure to control English fans.

Greenwood surprisingly selected Garry Birtles to partner his Forest teammate Tony Woodcock for the must-win match against Italy in place of David Johnson, who had a remarkable record of having scored six goals in seven internationals. Johnson was never on a losing England side (winning five of the eight games he played in). The hosts won, with a goal by Tardelli.

England completed their group results with a 2-1 win over Spain, who finished bottom. Brooking and Woodcock scored the goals to bring to an end one of the national side's poorest competition showings.

The group format of the finals did not prove to be a success and 12 games produced only 27 goals. The overall quality of the football and the refereeing of it was universally condemned by observers of the game across Europe. Some things would change in 1984.

'ITALY Here we come'

The England Players Official European Championship Brochure 1980

Articles by Ron Greenwood Kevin Keegan All England Players Featured International statistics

Price £1.00

Sponsored by PHILISHAVE

MOST DANGEROUS ENGLAND PLAYER

DAVID JOHNSON, who had six goals in seven appearances and had never been on a losing England team, played in the opener against Belgium. But he never played for England again.

MOST DANGEROUS OPPONENT

DINO ZOFF, who was to lift the World Cup two years later as Italy's captain, chose the group game in Turin to claim another clean sheet against England, a record fourth in six appearances against England. It is a record that still stands after more than a quarter of a century.

EUROPEAN CHAMPIONSHIPS 1980 QUALIFYING

GROUP 1 WINNERS: ENGLAND

England 1st P8/W7/D1/L0/F22/A5/PTS15

Denmark 3 [Simonsen, Rontved, Arnesen] v England 4 [Keegan (2), Latchford, Neal]

20 Sept 1978 (Copenhagen)

Rep Ireland 1 [Daly] v England 1 [Latchford]

25 Oct 1978 (Dublin)

England 4 [Keegan, Latchford (2), Watson] v N. Ireland 0

7 Feb 1979 (Wembley)

Bulgaria 0 v England 3 [Keegan, Watson, Barnes]

6 June 1979 (Sofia)

England 1 [Keegan] v Denmark 0

12 Sept 1979 (Wembley)

N. Ireland 1 [Moreland] v England 5 [Francis (2), Woodcock (2) Nicholl (o.g.)]

17 Oct 1979 (Belfast)

England 2 [Watson, Hoddle] v Bulgaria 0

22 Nov 1979 (Wembley)

England 2 [Keegan (2)] v Rep Ireland 0

6 Feb 1980 (Wembley)

EUROPEAN CHAMPIONSHIPS 1980 FINALS

GROUP B WINNERS BELGIUM

England 3rd P3/W1/D1/L1/F3/A3 eliminated

England 1 [Wilkins] v Belgium 1 [Ceulemans]

12 June 1980 (Turin)

Italy 1 [Tardelli] v England 0

15 June 1980 (Turin)

England 2 [Brooking, Woodcock] v Spain 1 [Dani]

18 June 1980 (Naples)

THE FINAL

Belgium 1 [Vandereycken] v West Germany 2 [Hrubesch (2)]

22 June 1980 (Rome)

BRITISH HOME INTERNATIONAL CHAMPIONSHIPS 1976–80

HOME INTERNATIONAL CHAMPIONSHIPS 1976

ENGLAND	P3	W2	D0	L1	F6	A2	GD4	PTS4

(Winners: Scotland. England 2nd)

Wales 0 v England 1 [Taylor]

8 May 1976 (Cardiff)

England 4 [Channon (2, I pen) Francis G, Pearson] v N. Ireland 0

11 May 1976 (Wembley)

Scotland 2 [Masson, Dalglish] v England 1 [Channon]

15 May 1976 (Hampden Park)

HOME INTERNATIONAL CHAMPIONSHIPS 1977

ENGLAND	P3	W1	D1	L1	F3	A4	GD1	PTS3

(Winners: Scotland. England 3rd)

N. Ireland 1 [McGrath] v England 2 [Channon, Tueart]

28 May 1977 (Belfast)

England 0 v Wales 1 [James L]

31 May 1977 (Wembley)

England 1 [Channon (pen)] v Scotland 2 [Masson, Dalglish]

4 June 1977 (Wembley)

HOME INTERNATIONAL CHAMPIONSHIPS 1978

ENGLAND	P3	W3	D0	L0	F5	A1	GD4	PTS6

(Winners: England)

Wales 1 [Dwyer] v England 3 [Barnes P, Currie, Latchford]

13 May 1978 (Cardiff)

England 1 [Neal (pen)] v N. Ireland 0

16 May 1978 (Wembley)

Scotland 0 v England 1 [Coppell]

20 May 1978 (Hampden Park)

HOME INTERNATIONAL CHAMPIONSHIPS 1979

ENGLAND	P3	W2	D1	L0	F5	A1	GD4	PTS5

(Winners: England)

N. Ireland 0 v England 2 [Watson D, Coppell]

19 May 1979 (Belfast)

England 0 v Wales 0

23 May 1979 (Wembley)

England 3 [Barnes P, Coppell, Keegan] v Scotland 1 [Wark]

25 May 1979 (Wembley)

England used 41 players in the 15 Home Internationals played in this period but only won the tournament twice. They also failed to qualify for either the European Championships (1976) or the World Cup in Argentina (1978). Don Revie resigned as manager before being sacked, in June 1977, and Ron Greenwood (whose West Ham team had thrashed Revie's Leeds a very satisfying 7-0 in 1966 at Upton Park) took over as temporary manager in August. He became full manager in December '77, too late to save the 1978 World Cup qualifying campaign, but with plenty of time to build toward the World Cup in Spain in 1982.

Less than a week after the Scotland game in 1976, England were in Los Angeles losing 1-0 to Brazil in their opening game of the USA Bicentennial Cup. They went on to beat Italy in New York 3-2, and Team America 3-1 in Philadelphia to end the tournament runners-up to the Brazilians. It was the best Revie would manage against world-class opposition during his time in charge.

As if to rub the English noses in it, the Scots – who qualified for the 1974 and now 1978 World Cup finals – won the Home Internationals Championships for the second year in a row in 1977. The Scottish fans made

HOME INTERNATIONAL CHAMPIONSHIPS 1980

ENGLAND	P3	W1	D1	L1	F4	A5	GD1	PTS3

(Winners: N. Ireland. England 2nd)

Wales 4 [Walsh, Thomas M, James L, Thompson (o.g.)] v England 1 [Mariner]

17 May 1980 (Wrexham)

England 1 [Johnson] v N. Ireland 1 [Cochrane]

20 May 1980 (Wembley)

Scotland 0 v England 2 [Brooking, Coppell]

24 May 1980 (Hampden Park)

FINAL TABLE HOME INTERNATIONAL CHAMPIONSHIPS 1976–80

	P	W	D	L	F	A	GD	PTS(/24)
England	12	7	3	2	17	11	6	17
Wales	12	4	5	3	13	9	4	13
Scotland	12	4	3	5	9	14	-5	11
N. Ireland	12	2	4	6	7	18	-11	6

their mark on Wembley, causing £18,000 worth of damage after watching their team win (which is £millions in today's money).

Ron Greenwood got England back to winning ways when he took charge of England after seeing them lose the British Championships to the Scots in May 1977 and they won the Home Internationals in 1978 and 1979.

There was a shock for England and Scotland, when in 1980 Northern Ireland won their first outright British title since 1914. They were helped in no small measure by Wales' 4-1 crushing of England at Wrexham and their own draw at Wembley.

PLAYERS USED BY ENGLAND

MANAGER: DON REVIE (1976–1977)
RON GREENWOOD (1978–1980)

GOALKEEPERS

Ray Clemence (Liverpool), Peter Shilton (Stoke City, Notts Forest/1978), Joe Corrigan (Man City)

DEFENDERS

Phil Neal (Liverpool), Dave Clement (QPR), Mick Mills (Ipswich), Tony Towers (Sunderland), Trevor Cherry (Leeds), Kenny Sansom (Crystal Palace), Phil Thompson (Liverpool), Colin Todd (Derby), Roy McFarland (Derby), Mike Doyle (Man City), Dave Watson (Man City), Emlyn Hughes (Liverpool), Larry Lloyd (Notts Forest)

MIDFIELDERS

Glenn Hoddle (Tottenham), Brian Greenhoff (Man Utd), Gerry Francis (QPR), Ray Kennedy (Liverpool), Peter Taylor (Crystal Palace), Ray Wilkins (Chelsea), Brian Talbot (Ipswich), Trevor Brooking (West Ham), Tony Currie (Sheff Utd), Steve Coppell (Man Utd), Peter Barnes (Man City), Terry McDermott (Liverpool), Laurie Cunningham (WBA), Alan Devonshire (West Ham)

FORWARDS

Kevin Keegan (Liverpool), Stuart Pearson (Man Utd), Joe Royle (Man City), Mick Channon (S'hampton), Paul Mariner (Ipswich), Trevor Francis (Birmingham, Notts Forest/1979), Dennis Tueart (Man City), Bob Latchford (Everton), Tony Woodcock (Notts Forest), Kevin Reeves (Man City), David Johnson (Ipswich, Liverpool/1976)

WORLD CUP SPAIN 1982

'GOTCHA!' (*THE SUN*, on sinking *The Belgrano*)
It was the age of the New Romantics and the bubbly perm had been replaced by the mullet on the terraces and pitches across the land. Everyone in England was becoming designer-aware in a big way. But while High Street clothes were getting bigger shoulders, more pleats and more ornamentation, England's strip was getting smaller and nastier. The shorts were almost obscene in their skimpiness and the stripes on the shirt were simply ludicrous. How could a player feel proud of representing his country in such a silly outfit?

Looking daft wasn't the only thing that the team, who had qualified along with Hungary from Group 4, despite having lost in Romania, Norway and Switzerland, had to deal with in the run-up to the finals, though. Even before the first game could kick off, the 1982 World Cup finals were dogged by controversy. In a typically convoluted January draw, the organising committee managed to have the wrong balls put into the wrong containers and when the first balls were drawn they were put into the wrong groups. When it was all sorted England were favourably lodged with France, Czechoslovakia and Kuwait.

Then, two months before the tournament began, the Falklands War kicked off without the whistle being blown. The Argentines invaded The Falklands, which was and remains a British dependency. Since the combatants had both seen their national football teams qualify for the World Cup there was a chance that they'd meet on the pitch as well as at Goose Green. English media and public opinion were divided as to whether England should go to the World Cup (although curiously they were in agreement that their soldiers should go to the Falklands: loss of life being so much less important than loss of a match, obviously). As it became clear that the Argentines were losing the War, the argument became redundant and the English would have at least one victory to celebrate in the summer of 1982.

What the best-dressed England fan was wearing in Spain 1982

The England (football) squad left for Spain on the back of an impressive run of six wins and a draw in which they conceded just two goals. It was no coincidence that the run came after Don Howe was appointed as coach and assistant to Ron Greenwood.

It was something of a surprise that England travelled to Spain with nine players the wrong side of 30 and several either carrying injuries or highly prone to them. The first game at the finals would be Ron

ENGLAND SQUAD

	CLUB	AGE	CAPS	GOALS
GOALKEEPERS				
Ray Clemence	Tottenham	33	58	
Peter Shilton	Notts Forest	32	37	
Joe Corrigan	Man City	33	9	
FULL BACKS				
Viv Anderson	Notts Forest	25	11	
Mick Mills	Ipswich	33	37	
Phil Neal	Liverpool	31	37	3
Kenny Sansom	Arsenal	23	23	
CENTRE BACKS				
Terry Butcher	Ipswich	23	4	
Steve Foster	Brighton	24	2	
Phil Thompson	Liverpool	28	38	1
MIDFIELD				
Trevor Brooking	West Ham	33	46	5
Steve Coppell	Man Utd	26	36	6
Glenn Hoddle	Tottenham	24	11	4
Terry McDermott	Liverpool	30	23	3
Graham Rix	Arsenal	24	8	
Bryan Robson	Man Utd	25	19	4
Ray Wilkins	Man Utd	25	47	3
FORWARDS				
Trevor Francis	Man City	28	27	6
Kevin Keegan	Liverpool	31	62	21
Paul Mariner	Ipswich	29	21	10
Peter Withe	Aston Villa	30	6	
Tony Woodcock	Notts Forest	26	22	7

Previous page: BACK L-R: Robson, Woodcock, Foster, Hoddle, Withe, Anderson, Brooking, Mariner, Wilkins. MIDDLE L-R: Street, Hurst, Rix, Thompson, Clemence, Corriga, Shilton, Butcher, Coppell, Howe, Medhurst. FRONT L-R: Sansom, McDermott, Keegan, Greenwood, Mills, Neal, Francis

THE MANAGER: RON GREENWOOD

After the final game in Spain, Greenwood resigned from the job of England manager. Apparently he'd told his players that he was going to resign on the plane back from their last qualifying game in Hungary, which they'd won 3-1, securing qualification for the finals. They persuaded him to stay until after the World Cup proper.

By the time of his retirement Greenwood had been manager for almost exactly five years and left the post with a win percentage only bettered by Ramsey and, later, Glenn Hoddle (and the latter only just beats Ron, by 60.71% to 59.99%) in the history of England managers (so far).

Also like Sir Alf, Ron is the only other England manager to end a World Cup unbeaten. (Well, it's something, right? No trophy won, but at least 'unbeaten'.) He tried to play entertaining football, liked his players to pass to each other at feet rather than launch it up and over a defence and his England tenure goal difference of +53 from 55 games (93 scored) is testament to his positive approach to the game.

A likeable man who perhaps came to the job too late in life, Ron Greenwood got England to both a European Championships, having rescued qualification from the jaws of defeat under Don Revie, and a World Cup finals, and England hadn't managed that for 12 years previously.

After retiring from the England job Greenwood retired from managing and became a BBC Radio pundit. He was awarded a CBE for services to the game in 1981.

Ron Greenwood died in February 2006 at the age of 84.

GREENWOOD'S ENGLAND RECORD 10 SEPT 1980 – 5 JULY 1982

P	W	D	L	F	A	WIN %
23	12	5	6	33	15	52.1

Greenwood's 50th in charge and to celebrate he dropped his skipper, Kevin Keegan. Despite being England's most potent striker, with a goal per game ratio better than one in three, Keegan was carrying a persistent back problem which would mean he'd finish his international career against Spain on 5 July 1982, having made a single appearance in a World Cup finals tournament as a substitute, on for only 26 minutes.

England made the best possible start to the competition when Bryan Robson scored after 27 seconds against France. That goal stood as the fastest ever until Davor Sukur reduced it to just four seconds in 2002. France equalised with their first goal in four games but Robson restored the lead with a header. Paul Mariner then equalled Jimmy Greaves' feat of 1961 by scoring for his fifth consecutive international game. Phil Neal replaced Sansom late on and won his first cap without touching the ball.

For the first time in three years an unchanged England team took the field against Czechoslovakia. Trevor Francis hooked home his seventh international goal after an hour, and a Barmos own goal meant

Every schoolboy in 1982 wanted to be one of these players. Except maybe Peter Withe. Or Terry McDermott ('Eh youse, calm down now, calm down')

WHY WAS HE THERE?

PETER WITHE was a typically direct and bruising English centre forward of the old type. In six internationals the Villa man did not find the net once. In 35 Division One games he scored 10 for his club. The fact that he didn't play a single minute in Spain leads one to ask the question of why was he there? His reluctance to adapt sartorially to the times should have seen his omission from the squad, what with that facial hair and unruly mop on his head, Withe could never be as cool as Hoddle, Wilkins or John Barnes.

WHY WASN'T HE THERE?

JOHN BARNES. He was only 17 at the time of the 1982 World Cup, but he'd just played a big part in Watford's promotion to Division One in 1981–82 and in a few years time England would revel in discovering fresh, young talent at World Cups (see Michael Owen and Wayne Rooney). Barnes was strong, fast and skilful and would have been a complete surprise to all opposition at the finals. His youth and inexperience could well have been an asset too, since he was less likely to be afraid of failing and little would have been expected of him.

England had won their two opening games, for the first time in a World Cup finals. Paul Mariner tried to claim England's second goal and so beat Jimmy Greaves' record. Jimmy, covering the finals as a TV pundit, wryly commented that 'if he's claiming that, then I want to amend my scoring record by several hundred'.

In the final group game against Kuwait Steve Foster became the first Brighton player, and first in a silly headband, to win an England cap, replacing Butcher who was on a yellow card, while Hoddle deputised for the injured Robson (groin) and Neal filled in for Mick Mills. A scrappy game was won by Trevor Francis and England ended the first round as winners of Group 4. Which meant that they would play the Second Round in Group B, with West Germany and hosts Spain.

Having started so well against France, England had

Ray 'Butch' Wilkins celebrates winning the award of most overrated English player from me. Paul Mariner whispers well done in his ear

then scored fewer goals in each successive game as the tournament progressed and a 0-0 result against West Germany was almost predictable. When the Germans beat the hosts it left England needing a winning margin over Spain of two goals or better, or by one goal in a high-scoring game (3-2 or greater).

Spain were already out and England would soon join them. Just as with their last World Cup game in 1970 when the manager was castigated for his substitutions, so too was Greenwood for his. When he finally sent Brooking and Keegan into the fray they proved the pick of the England players, especially Brooking. Which begged the question of why he didn't start. Not that either he or Keegan could change the game, which

MOST OVERRATED ENGLAND PLAYER

RAY WILKINS was a clever and sophisticated midfielder who should have been at home amidst the culture of international football. However, he rarely affected or changed games with the decisive pass or killer goal, as a record of just three in 47 England games, going into the 1982 World Cup, showed.

MOST DANGEROUS ENGLAND PLAYER

BRYAN ROBSON. The tabloids called him Captain Marvel and despite his tendency to break bits of himself because of being over-committed to his game, Robson would always look to lead his team with determination and a will to win that was second to none. He was joint top scorer for England with two goals, but they were both against difficult opposition in Spain while the other joint top scorer, Trevor Francis, who was a striker, scored one against Kuwait. Paolo Rossi finished the tournament as top scorer with six in seven games.

MOST DANGEROUS OPPONENT

RON GREENWOOD. He believed that he couldn't play either Keegan or Brooking, his most influential players, because of injury. But when he needed a win over Spain by two clear goals he waited until it was too late to put both on as subs. In his autobiography Keegan later claimed that both he and Brooking were fit and that not playing the two was 'Ron Greenwood's biggest mistake'.

WORLD CUP 1982 RESULTS

FIRST ROUND GROUP 4 WINNERS: ENGLAND

England P3/W3/D0/L0/F6/A1
England 3 [Robson (2), Mariner] v France 1 [Soler]
16 June 1982 (Bilbao)
England 2 [Francis, Barmos (o.g.)] v Czechoslovakia 0
20 June 1982 (Bilbao)
England 1 [Francis] v Kuwait 0
25 June 1982 (Bilbao)

SECOND ROUND GROUP B WINNERS: WEST GERMANY

England 2nd P2/W0/D2/L0/F0/A0
West Germany 0 v England 0
29 June 1982 (Madrid)
Spain 0 v England 0
5 July 1982 (Madrid)

THE FINAL

Italy 3 [Rossi, Tardelli, Albotelli] v West Germany 1 [Breitner]
11 July 1982 (Madrid)

ended goalless. Which wasn't a defeat, either.

England went out unbeaten while France (beaten by England) lost to West Germany (who had drawn with England) in the semi-final. Italy beat the Germans in the final. The Italian strip worn that day was rather nice, as you'd expect, and it made fashion-conscious fans slightly glad that the dreadful England strip was not seen on the same pitch as the winners.

WHERE'S GEOFF?

By now Geoff Hurst MBE (awarded in 1975), he was at the competition, with England. His old manager Ron Greenwood hired him as an assistant coach in 1977 (when Geoff was player-coach at part-time Telford United). Greenwood thought that Geoff's presence would help inspire a new generation of players to World Cup success. Chelsea hired Geoff as manager in 1979 but sadly were not capable of winning anything, and he couldn't prevent relegation in 1979 to the Second Division. After finishing 4th the next season, Chelsea could only make 12th in 1980–81 and Geoff was sacked, in April 1981.

EUROPEAN CHAMPIONSHIPS FRANCE 1984

Ron Greenwood quit as England manager after his team's exit from the World Cup in Spain in July 1982. Bobby Robson's appointment was made almost immediately, but he didn't start until September. His first game was a European qualifier away to Denmark and only a last-minute Jesper Olsen equaliser to end it 2-2 made it a less than perfect beginning. After the almost obligatory manager's try-out against West Germany, in a friendly that England lost 2-1 at Wembley, Robson's team won their next three games; two qualifiers for Euro '84 and a Home International. Then, in March 1983, they failed to beat Greece at Wembley, and while they beat Hungary next game, a loss to Denmark at home in September did for them.

MOST DANGEROUS ENGLAND PLAYER

TONY WOODCOCK was that rarity in English football, a thinking striker. Unlike most of his ilk, Tony could involve himself in passing movements, not just be a finisher of them. He proved that by making the transition from the First Division in England to the Bundesliga for a new German transfer record of £500,000 in 1979 and in 81 games scored 28 times. He had a strike ratio for England of better than a goal every three games.

MOST DANGEROUS OPPONENT

ALLAN SIMONSEN of Denmark proved to be a player England could not cope with, floating as he did between striker and midfield. Apart from the crucial goal he scored to beat England at Wembley, Simonsen is still the only footballer to score in each of the three major European club finals, the European Cup, European Cup Winners Cup and UEFA Cup.

MOST OVERRATED ENGLAND PLAYER

LUTHER BLISSETT is one of those particular players English football throws up from time to time. Outstanding for his club side, Watford, but less so outside Vicarage Road, his home ground. He scored a hat-trick against Luxembourg but should have set a new scoring record considering the chances he had. Those three were the only goals he netted in 14 England appearances. They helped secure Luther an unlikely transfer to AC Milan, where despite scoring just five goals in 30 appearances in 1983–84, he became a cult hero and his name is today used by an arts collective to disguise their true identity when staging exhibitions or writing novels.

EUROPEAN CHAMPIONSHIPS 1984 QUALIFYING

GROUP 2 WINNERS: DENMARK

England 2nd P8/W5/D2/L1/F23/A3 (did not qualify)

Denmark 2 [Hansen (pen), Olsen] v England 2 [Francis T (2)]

22 Sept 1982 (Copenhagen)

Greece 0 v England 3 [Woodcock 2, Lee]

17 Nov 1982 (Salonika)

England 9 [Blissett (3), Woodcock, Coppell, Hoddle, Chamberlain, Neal, Bossi (o.g.)] v Luxembourg 0

15 Dec 1982 (Wembley)

England 0 v Greece 0

30 Mar 1983 (Wembley)

England 2 [Francis, Withe] v Hungary 0

27 April 1983 (Wembley)

England 0 v Denmark 1 [Simonsen (pen)]

21 Sept 1983 (Wembley)

Hungary 0 v England 3 [Hoddle, Lee, Mariner]

12 Oct 1983 (Budapest)

Luxembourg 0 v England 4 [Robson (2), Mariner, Butcher]

16 Nov 1983 (Luxembourg)

TO BE OR NOT TO BE

Robson later admitted that he sent his selection out for the Denmark game after planting negativity in the minds of his players with his pre-match pep-talk, which centred on the talents of the opposing players.

Denmark confounded all expectations by playing for a win. And with Brian Laudrup and Allan Simonsen dominant they did so with a penalty, just before the interval, after Phil Neal handled. It was a first win over England in nine attempts and sent Denmark through to the finals (they lost a semi-final to Spain).

The tournament was won by France in Paris, after beating Spain 2-0 (Platini and Bellone).

PLAYERS USED BY ENGLAND

	CLUB	AGE	CAPS	GOALS
GOALKEEPERS				
Peter Shilton	Notts Forest	32	42	
Ray Clemence	Liverpool	33	59	
FULL BACKS				
Phil Neal	Liverpool	31	39	3
Michael Duxbury	Man Utd	23	1st	
Kenny Sansom	Arsenal	24	27	
John Gregory	QPR	28	4	
CENTRE BACKS				
Russell Osman	Ipswich Town	23	6	
Terry Butcher	Ipswich Town	24	8	
Alvin Martin	West Ham	24	4	
Gary Mabbutt	Tottenham	22	1	
MIDFIELDERS				
Ricky Hill	Luton	24		
Sammy Lee	Liverpool	23		
Bryan Robson	Man Utd	26	23	6
Steve Coppell	Man Utd	26	40	6
Glenn Hoddle	Tottenham	25	13	4
Graham Rix	Arsenal	25	13	
Alan Devonshire	West Ham	26	6	
Ray Wilkins	Man Utd	26	52	3
John Barnes	Watford	20	4	
FORWARDS				
Paul Mariner	Ipswich Town	31	26	11
Mark Chamberlain	Stoke City	21		
Tony Woodcock	FC Cologne	28	25	8
Tony Morley	Aston Villa	28	4	
Luther Blissett	Watford	24	1	
Peter Withe	Aston Villa	32	6	
Trevor Francis	Sampdoria	28	32	8
Gordon Cowans	Aston Villa	24	1	

BRITISH HOME INTERNATIONAL CHAMPIONSHIPS 1981–84

HOME INTERNATIONAL CHAMPIONSHIPS 1981

ENGLAND	P2	W0	D1	L1	F0	A1	GD1	PTS1

(No winners, series uncompleted)

England 0 v Wales 0

20 May 1981 (Wembley)

England 0 v Scotland 1 [Robertson (pen)]

23 May 1981 (Wembley)

HOME INTERNATIONAL CHAMPIONSHIPS 1982

ENGLAND	P3	W3	D0	L0	F6	A0	GD6	PTS9

(Winners: England)

England 4 [Robson, Keegan, Wilkins, Hoddle] v N. Ireland 0

23 Feb 1982 (Wembley)

Wales 0 v England 1 [Francis T]

27 April 1982 (Cardiff)

Scotland 0 v England 1 [Mariner]

29 May 1982 (Hampden Park)

HOME INTERNATIONAL CHAMPIONSHIPS 1983

ENGLAND	P3	W2	D1	L0	F4	A1	GD3	PTS7

(Winners: England)

England 2 [Butcher, Neal (pen)] v Wales 1 [Rush]

23 Feb 1983 (Wembley)

N. Ireland 0 v England 0

28 May 1983 (Belfast)

England 2 [Robson, Cowans] v Scotland 0

1 June 1983 (Wembley)

HOME INTERNATIONAL CHAMPIONSHIPS 1984

ENGLAND	P3	W1	D1	L1	F2	A2	GD0	PTS4

(Winners: N. Ireland. England 3rd)

England 1 [Woodcock] v N. Ireland 0

4 April 1984 (Wembley)

Wales 1 [Hughes M] v England 0

2 May 1984 (Wrexham)

Scotland 1 [McGhee] v England 1 [Woodcock]

26 May 1984 (Hampden Park)

The Home International Championships just about reached their 1984 centenary, but with only the England–Scotland fixture attracting anything like a decent crowd – and they were not always there for the football.

With the threat from hooligans blighting the national game the Football Association banned ticket sales to supporters from Scotland for the 1981 fixture. The FA was taken to court by the Scottish Supporters' Club citing the Race Relations Act (they failed). An estimated 50,000 Scots 'invaded' London for the game anyway. It was probably a good thing the 1981 Championships were not completed (the troubles in Northern Ireland meant that both England and Wales refused to play there), since World Cup qualification was in doubt after England drew and then lost to Romania in 1981. Losing to Scotland in May meant that for the first time ever, England went four consecutive games without scoring.

At the beginning of the 1980–81 season the Football League made it three points for a win instead of the traditional two.

Ron Greenwood having retired after his team's elimination from the World Cup in Spain (where at least they'd not lost to West Germany) in 1982, new manager Bobby Robson started with a draw and two wins in

FINAL TABLE BRITISH HOME INTERNATIONAL CHAMPIONSHIPS 1982–84

	P	W	D	L	F	A	GD	PTS(/27)
England	9	6	2	1	12	3	9	20
Scotland	9	3	3	3	7	8	-1	12
Wales	9	3	1	5	8	9	-1	10
N. Ireland	9	1	4	4	4	11	-7	7

European Championships qualifiers (v Denmark, Greece, and Luxemburg in Sept, Oct and Nov 1982) but suffered a friendly loss at Wembley to the Germans in only his second game in charge. He was in charge for the 1983 Home Internationals, though, which England won. By the end of November 1982 the rule that required players to be sent off for committing a professional foul had seen 120 players dismissed. And the International FA Board had passed a rule that goalkeepers had to release the ball after taking four steps while holding it.

While the 89th and final British Championships ended with Tony Woodcock's stunning goal that earned England a draw in Scotland, the result gave the British Championships to Northern Ireland, on goal difference from Wales. The English and Scottish FAs had announced that they would be withdrawing from the tournament and so it ended – with both teams bottom.

A year later it all went wrong for English clubs in Europe. In the 1985 European Cup Final, Liverpool fans charged the supporters of opponents Juventus at the Heysel Stadium, resulting in 39 deaths when a wall collapsed on the retreating fans. As a consequence English clubs were banned from European competition for five years and Liverpool for six.

So that was no European football for English clubs and no more Home Internationals, either. Would the lack of 'distraction' then make England a stronger international team? Is the Pope Jewish?

PLAYERS USED BY ENGLAND

THE MANAGER: RON GREENWOOD (1980–1982)
THE MANAGER: BOBBY ROBSON (1983–1984)

GOALKEEPERS

Joe Corrigan (Man City), Ray Clemence (Liverpool), Peter Shilton (Notts Forest, S'hampton/1982)

DEFENDERS

Mick Mills (Ipswich), Viv Anderson (Notts Forest, Arsenal/1984), Kenny Sansom (Arsenal), Phil Neal (Liverpool), Derek Staham (WBA), Alan Kennedy (Liverpool), Micky Duxbury (Man Utd), Dave Watson (Werder Bremen, S'hampton/1980), Alvin Martin (West Ham), Steve Foster (Brighton), Phil Thompson (Liverpool), Terry Butcher (Ipswich), Graham Roberts (Tottenham), Terry Fenwick (QPR), Mark Wright (S'hampton)

MIDFIELDERS

Bryan Robson (Man Utd), Ray Wilkins (Man Utd, AC Milan/1984), Steve Coppell (Man Utd), Glenn Hoddle (Tottenham), Graham Rix (Arsenal), Peter Barnes (Man City), Tony Morley (Aston Villa), Terry McDermott (Liverpool), Trevor Brooking (West Ham), John Gregory (QPR), Steve Hunt (WBA), John Barnes (Watford), Sammy Lee (Liverpool)

FORWARDS

Paul Mariner (Ipswich, Arsenal/1984), Cyril Regis (WBA), Peter Withe (Aston Villa), Tony Woodcock (FC Cologne, Arsenal/1982), Trevor Francis (Notts Forest, Man City/1981), Kevin Keegan (S'hampton), Paul Walsh (Luton), Luther Blissett (Watford, AC Milan/1983), David Armstrong (S'hampton), Mark Chamberlain (Stoke), Gary Lineker (Leicester)

1986

'IT WAS THE HAND OF GOD' (DIEGO MARADONA)

Mexico 1986 was a mammoth competition. Fifty-two matches were scheduled for the hottest month of the year in the first country to host the finals twice (they got it after Colombia withdrew). It took two weeks and 36 matches just to eliminate eight countries and the fact that games were played at midday, to accommodate television broadcasts, was seen as an unfair advantage to those nations used to such conditions. At least, it was seen that way by the English press.

England had qualified as unbeaten group winners, two points ahead of Northern Ireland after eight games. If they'd reached the final itself, they would have played a total of 15 games, which was a third of a domestic

Obviously the referee was unsighted, there's no way that he could see the handball from where he was. Or maybe God had blinded him temporarily?

ENGLAND SQUAD

	CLUB	AGE	CAPS	GOALS
GOALKEEPERS				
Peter Shilton	S'hampton	36	81	
Chris Woods	Norwich	26	4	
Gary Bailey	Man Utd	27		
FULL BACKS				
Gary Stevens	Everton	23	9	
Kenny Sansom	Arsenal	27	65	1
Viv Anderson	Arsenal	29	20	1
CENTRE BACKS				
Alvin Martin	West Ham	27	16	1
Terry Butcher	Ipswich	27	40	3
Terry Fenwick	QPR	26	2	
Gary A Stevens	Tottenham	24	5	
MIDFIELDERS				
Glenn Hoddle	Tottenham	28	33	8
Bryan Robson	Man Utd	29	51	18
Ray Wilkins	AC Milan	29	82	3
Peter Reid	Everton	29	6	
Trevor Steven	Everton	22	10	3
Steve Hodge	Aston Villa	23	3	
FORWARDS				
Mark Hateley	AC Milan	24	18	9
Gary Lineker	Everton	25	13	6
Chris Waddle	Tottenham	25	16	2
John Barnes	Watford	22	27	3
Peter Beardsley	Newcastle	25	5	1
Kerry Dixon	Chelsea	24	6	4

Previous page: BACK L-R: Dixon, Waddle, Stevens, Hately, Woods, Bailey, Hoddle, Anderson, Barnes. MIDDLE L-R: Wilkins, Shilton, Fenwick, Sansom, Hodge, Beardsley, Butcher. FRONT L-R: Unknown, Robson B, Kenneth Baker (Tory minister), Millichip, Unknown, Robson R at an FA reception before flying to Spain

THE MANAGER: BOBBY ROBSON

When he took over as manager from Ron Greenwood, Bobby Robson seemed to be quite optimistic about his chances, stating that, 'I know I'm the best man for the job.' Though he did admit later that, 'When I took over I was a million miles away from understanding the unique demands of the job.'

Even if he never did come to terms with the special requirements needed for an England manager, he was really quite successful.

After handing the captaincy of the team to Bryan Robson and dispensing with Kevin Keegan's services altogether on taking the job, Robson was soon accused of being a ditherer, before, during and after matches – did he, asked media and fans alike, actually know who would be in his 'first' team? Yet although Robson's biggest reverse in his first year with England was the home defeat to Denmark in the 1983 European Championships qualifier (1-0 in September 1983), he never again lost a qualifying game, of which there were 22 in all.

The second year of Robson's tenure was very poor. After England failed to reach Euro '84 they were beaten by Wales in the final Home International competition (4-0!) and lost 2-0 to USSR at Wembley. The only bright spot was a first ever win in Brazil, when an amazing John Barnes solo goal helped England win 2-0. That win inspired England, and they swept through the qualifying tournament for the 1986 World Cup to finish top of their group, unbeaten.

ROBSON'S ENGLAND RECORD 22 SEPT 1982 – 22 JUNE 1986

P	W	D	L	F	A	WIN %
44	24	11	9	67	22	54.5

(Note: Ten of the wins were in friendlies and only four of the defeats were in competitive games)

BRYAN ROBSON. While there was no question of Robbo not going to the finals, he should have stayed on the subs bench (from where he could at least motivate the team). He was arguably the best midfielder England has ever had, being able to tackle, pass accurately and over distance, plus he provided the massive bonus of scoring goals regularly. But he went to Mexico having missed half a season with a dislocated shoulder which required surgery. He also had a hamstring injury which prevented proper training.

season's worth of games. Sky Sports might not yet exist, but clearly FIFA were expecting some serious TV revenues to start coming in soon. The 1986 World Cup is still the only finals in which England were not seeded as a top team. However the draw (apparently) favoured them for the opening round. Bobby Robson's team dominated the Group F opener against Portugal (playing their first finals since 1966) but couldn't score.

GOD. The English one, that is, not the South American, Argentinian-supporting God who leant Maradona a hand to score the first 'goal' against England. Maybe it was England's own fault, what with Church attendances in terminal decline, schools no longer obliged to have morning assemblies at which prayers are offered and hymns sung, vicars wearing their hair long and playing guitars in pulpits. It wasn't like that in Argentina. Clearly, God preferred his worship done the South American way.

Peter Shilton was just 15 minutes away from creating a new record of keeping five consecutive clean sheets in finals when the Portuguese scored with their first attack. It was England's first defeat of the year and a first reverse in 15 World Cup games. It was also Portugal's only win in Mexico and they were destined to finish bottom of the group, with their disgruntled players going on strike between their next two games and refusing to train. The Portuguese squad objected to having to undergo too much altitude training, to not being allowed to cross over into the USA to shop, that there were too many press people in their uncomfortable hotel and that they were not being paid to advertise Adidas on their training shorts (so they wore them inside out). What would Ronaldo have made of it all, one wonders?

Despite Bryan Robson carrying a troubled hamstring, Bobby Robson fielded an unchanged side against Morocco, knowing that even an unthinkable defeat would not rule out progress, thanks to the confused qualification process. England started badly and got worse. Bryan Robson dislocated his troublesome shoulder and was ruled out of the tournament. He passed the captain's armband to Ray Wilkins, who was promptly sent off for throwing down a ball petulantly, after being penalised when he felt he had been fouled. The ball hit the ref, the ref hit his red card and Peter Shilton was hit with the armband and became England's third captain inside two minutes. Wilkins' dismissal was the first of an England player in World Cup finals and really should have been more dramatic – a scything tackle maybe, or a head-butt on an opponent. But no, it was a flounce. England's 10 men hung on to earn a draw, and a win against Poland in the last group game would ensure progress for England.

Despite pleas from Bryan Robson to play wearing a shoulder harness (isn't that a Monty Python sketch?), manager Bobby Robson dropped him and set about the Poles with a cautious 4-4-2 formation. A Gary Lineker hat-trick inside the first 35 minutes, England's first in a finals since Hurst's, claimed second place in the group and a second-round meeting with Paraguay.

Without Robson or Wilkins, Glenn Hoddle played in the centre of midfield for England against the Paraguayans and had a hand in all three goals, two from Lineker and one from Peter Beardsley.

England had started to play well and score goals, but they were drawn in the quarter-finals against Argentina, who were led by Maradona, a genuinely gifted footballer who was also not bad at basketball (especially given his size).

Diego Maradona is perhaps the only footballer who can be comfortably compared to Pelé. His stocky stature belied his nimbleness and turn of pace – although watching the five England players who failed to catch him as he went on a run through their ranks to score a second, decisive, goal against them, gives you a pretty good idea of both.

After the game Steve Hodge (remember him?) swapped shirts with Maradona, which was the closest any England player got to him on the day. Ho ho.

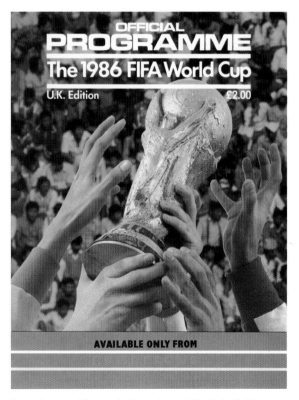

Strangely, none of the arms in this photo are clad in England shirts

MOST DANGEROUS OPPONENT

DIEGO MARADONA who had a (cheating) hand in England's exit, but didn't really need to, since he was the most extraordinarily gifted football player to appear since Pelé. As his second goal against England proved, he could waltz through defences, spray passes with ease and inspire his teammates to great heights of achievement. Plus he helped Argentina beat the Germans in the final.

MOST DANGEROUS ENGLAND PLAYER

GARY LINEKER finished Mexico '86 as winner of The Golden Boot for being the top scorer. He hit six of England's seven goals in the tournament, including a hat-trick against Poland, two against Paraguay and a consolation against Argentina. It would have been interesting to see how he might have improved his 12 goals in 18 internationals ratio had Maradona's hand not intervened.

MOST OVERRATED ENGLAND PLAYER

CHRIS WADDLE was like many of the wide men who have played for England. Hugely talented, he was one of the few England players who could carry the ball at pace, past an opponent. But when the team needed a flash of inspiration from him to turn a game or rescue a situation, it rarely came. Rubbish at penalties, too. And what about that mullet?

Later, Maradona attributed the first goal against England to The Hand of God. The same hand went on to lift the 1986 World Cup in a final that pitted the last two nations defeated by the Brits in a War against each other. For the watching dozens of football fans in England it must have been a close call as to who to support, Argentina or West Germany. Personally I thought that Rudi Voller's horrible mullet and worse moustache tipped the balance south of the equator.

WORLD CUP 1986 FINALS

GROUP F WINNERS MOROCCO

England 2nd P3/W1/D1/L1/F3/A1

Portugal 1 [Carlos Manuel] v England 0

3 June 1986 (Monterrey)

Morocco 0 v England 0

6 June 1986 (Monterrey)

Poland 0 v England 3 [Lineker (3)]

3 June 1986 (Monterrey)

ROUND OF 16

England 3 [Lineker (2), Beardsley] v Paraguay 0

18 June 1986 (Mexico City)

QUARTER-FINALS

Argentina 2 [Maradona (2)] v England 1 [Lineker]

22 June 1986 (Mexico City)

THE FINAL

Argentina 3 [Brown, Valdano, Burruchaga] v West Germany 2 [Rummenigge, Voller]

29 June 1986 (Mexico City)

WHERE'S GEOFF?

He had left the England set-up with Greenwood and, with no offers from other clubs, Geoff left football altogether and went into the insurance business, selling policies to car sales garages across the country. Twenty years after scoring the only hat-trick in a World Cup Final, Geoff Hurst was banging on people's doors to ask if he could sell them insurance. Which often went well, although one particular garage owner told him that he didn't buy things 'from ex-footballers'. Sir Geoff's story is very well told in his autobiography *1966 And All That*.

EUROPEAN CHAMPIONSHIPS
WEST GERMANY 1988

'THE FIRST 90 MINUTES ARE THE MOST IMPORTANT' (BOBBY ROBSON)

Two years earlier England had lost only one game at the group stage of the World Cup in Mexico (to Portugal) before going out against eventual winners Argentina in the quarter-finals. It was the best performance by England in a major tournament since Mexico in 1970. They hadn't lost a competitive game since the '86 World Cup (except friendlies away to Sweden and West Germany), although they had drawn seven out of 16 games going into the finals in West Germany.

So when they produced arguably their worst showing in an international tournament, losing all their games and finishing bottom of their group at the 1988 European Championships, it seemed as if the national game was going backwards, again.

It can be argued (and was, endlessly) that key players were either out or knackered and their replacements were woefully short in deputising.

Terry Butcher suffered a broken leg, Gary Lineker was eventually diagnosed with hepatitis, Waddle was not the player he'd been pre-hernia operation and the Liverpool pair of Barnes and Beardsley were exhausted after a tiring club season. And yet, surely Ireland, Holland and Russia were all beatable, weren't they?

Clearly not. Ironically England's downfall in the competition was due to the efforts of one of the Heroes of '66. Having been rejected as manager by his own country, Jack Charlton had become manager of the Republic of Ireland and had inspired them to great

In a scene reminiscent of *Lawrence of Arabia*, Bobby Robson (seated on an FA-funded taxi) prepares to conquer the foe leading a band of brigands

ENGLAND SQUAD

	CLUB	AGE	CAPS	GOALS
GOALKEEPERS				
Peter Shilton	Derby	38	98	
Chris Woods	Rangers	28	12	
FULL BACKS				
Gary M Stevens	Everton	25	23	
Kenny Sansom	Arsenal	29	83	1
Tony Dorigo	Chelsea	22		
Viv Anderson	Man Utd	31	29	2
CENTRAL DEFENDERS				
Dave Watson	Everton	26	11	
Tony Adams	Arsenal	21	11	2
Mark Wright	Derby	24	20	
MIDFIELDERS				
Glenn Hoddle	Monaco	29	50	8
Neil Webb	Man Utd	24	7	1
Trevor Steven	Everton	24	22	3
Chris Waddle	Tottenham	27	34	4
Bryan Robson	Man Utd	31	66	21
Steve McMahon	Liverpool	26	3	
Peter Reid	Everton	31	13	
FORWARDS				
John Barnes	Liverpool	24	39	6
Peter Beardsley	Liverpool	27	24	5
Mark Hateley	Monaco	27	28	9
Gary Lineker	Barcelona	27	32	26

Previous page: BACK L-R: Dorigo, Barnes, Watson, Hoddle, Hately, Adams, Waddle, Anderson, Stevens. MIDDLE L-R: Dr Crane (team doctor), Mike Kelly (GK coach), Robson R, Woods, Shilton, Seaman, Howe, Street (Physio), Medhurst (Physio). FRONT L-R: Steven, McMahon, Wright, Lineker, Robson B, Sansom, Webb, Beardsley, Reid

THE MANAGER: BOBBY ROBSON

Bobby Robson was a true football fan. If he couldn't take part in a game, then he'd love nothing better than watching one, which is probably why most of the players who played for him respected the man. Not as cerebral as Ron Greenwood, he was more honest than Don Revie and as patriotic as Sir Alf Ramsey. Yet his man-management skills were comparable to no previous England manager. He wasn't imperious, dictatorial or stand off-ish. He didn't insist on his players reading piles of reports on his opponents, although he certainly wanted to be prepared for whatever they might throw at him. He was brave enough to discard former English fans' favourites in his squads such as Kevin Keegan and include 'flair' players who might run into *cul de sacs* on the pitch, as long as they went past opponents to get there.

His publicly uttered malapropisms could undermine his authority at times: 'They're two points ahead of us so we're neck and neck', and 'He's very fast and if he gets a yard ahead of himself nobody will catch him', being two such examples. But his ability to get good enough results with England, combined with what seemed to be a gentle levelling off of public expectation for the national team to achieve anything that might earn them a trophy, seemed to keep him in the job until he could go out on a high. The 1988 European Championships were certainly not that high, though.

ROBSON'S ENGLAND RECORD 23 JUNE 1986 – 11 JUNE 1988

P	W	D	L	F	A	WIN %
17	8	7	2	30	11	44.5

(Note: The two defeats were in friendly away games in Sweden and West Germany)

WHY WAS HE THERE?

NEIL WEBB went to Euro '88 with seven caps and one goal to his international credit, although he was probably included in the squad on the back of his 47 goals for Forest in 146 appearances. Sadly for Webb his eight in 75 during his spell at Manchester United were a reflection of his unfortunate tendency to pick up long-term injuries.

WHY WASN'T HE THERE?

TONY COTTEE. He had his best ever season, scoring 29 goals during 1986–87, and added 15 in 1987–88. Had he been in Germany he might have been the ideal replacement for a struggling Gary Lineker who was suffering (undiagnosed) with hepatitis.

things. He'd begun by going to the extremes of UEFA's selection policy (one often-told joke at the time was that a player only need read *The Irish Times* to play for the country), but with a collection of Football League players and a core of Liverpool stars, Ireland humbled England 1-0 in the opening game. Glasgow-born Ray Houghton, nurtured in England, headed his first goal in 16 internationals (only the second headed goal of his professional career), to claim victory. It then got worse for England, on and off the field. The genius of Van Basten, who hit a hat-trick, and Ruud Gullit's

magnificent passing spoiled Peter Shilton's 100th cap.

Off the field, riots involving fans from England, Holland and Russia led to the Football Association withdrawing a request to UEFA to remove the ban on English clubs competing in European competitions.

If anything it was the third defeat, 3-1 by Russia, that best summed up the humiliation of Euro '88, and led to a vicious written assault on Bobby Robson in the tabloids. However, the FA stood by their manager as he set about the task of preparing for the qualifying campaign for the 1990 World Cup, to be held in Italy.

MOST DANGEROUS ENGLAND PLAYER

JACK CHARLTON. He'd won the World Cup more than twenty years earlier; he'd won League titles and FA Cups with Leeds Utd. And now as a manager he took a tiny nation into a major competition and got them to a better finishing spot than England managed. He also uncovered a wealth of neglected talent in the English game, best epitomised by Ray Houghton, and made them internationals of quality.

MOST DANGEROUS OPPONENT

MARCO VAN BASTEN, who showed England how football should be played and went on to help Holland deservedly win the tournament by beating USSR. Van Basten scored the winner in the final with a volley that is widely considered one of the best goals ever. He ended the competition as top scorer, with five — three more than the next highest scorers and four more than the highest-scoring Englishmen, Bryan Robson and Tony Adams. He was European Player of The Year in 1988 (and 1989, and 1992 when he was also voted World Player of the Year). In a cruelly short career he scored 118 goals in 280 games at club level and 24 in 58 for Holland.

MOST OVERRATED ENGLISH PLAYER

GLENN HODDLE was an irritating combination of sublime skill and inconsistency of performance at international level. So much so that his England manager, Bobby Robson, wondered publicly at one point 'if he was a luxury, whether we can afford to play him'. Years later Robson didn't include him in his Dream Team selection for his autobiography and kept silent on what he thought of Hoddle's use of a psychic healer at England camps.

EUROPEAN CHAMPIONSHIPS 1988 QUALIFYING

GROUP 4 WINNERS: ENGLAND

England P6/W5/D1/L0/F19/A1

England 3 [Lineker (2) Waddle] v N. Ireland 0

15 Oct 1986 (Wembley)

England 2 [Anderson, Mabbutt] v Yugoslavia 0

12 Nov 1986 (Wembley)

N. Ireland 0 v England 2 [Robson, Waddle]

29 April 1987 (Belfast)

Turkey 0 v England 0

29 April 1987 (Izmir)

England 8 [Lineker (3) Barnes (2) Robson, Beardsley, Webb] v Turkey 0

14 Oct 1987 (Wembley)

Yugoslavia 1 [Katanec] v England 4 [Beardsley, Barnes, Robson, Adams]

11 Nov 1987 (Belgrade)

EUROPEAN CHAMPIONSHIPS 1988 FINALS

GROUP B WINNERS: USSR

England 4th P3/W0/D0/L3/F2/A7 (eliminated)

England 0 v Rep Ireland 1 [Houghton]

12 June 1988 (Stuttgart)

England 1 [Robson] v Holland 3 [Van Basten (3)]

15 June 1988 (Dusseldorf)

England 1 [Adams] v USSR 3 [Aleinikov, Pasulko, Mikhailichenko]

18 June 1988 (Frankfurt)

THE FINAL

USSR 0 v 2 Holland [Gullit, Van Basten]

25 June 1988 (Munich)

WORLD CUP ITALY 1990

'TEARS WE GO...' [THE *SUN*]

As one of the losing quarter-finalists in the 1986 World Cup, England hoped for, and became, a seeded team for Italia '90. They did so at the expense of Spain, the other nation in contention for the last favoured slot. Despite having the better finals record, English fans swung it for our boys – security considerations won the day – and England were shuttled away to Sardinia.

Fate conspired to group England with two teams that had beaten them in the 1988 Euro Championships, Ireland and Holland. With the fanatical Dutch fans regarded as even worse than English hooligans, UEFA and the British government braced itself for any backlash against trouble that could lead to a reversal of the governing body's decision to readmit English clubs to European competition the following year.

The fact that England had gone through the qualifying group unbeaten, without conceding a goal, generated optimistic home support. However, the squad itself was bereft of any truly world-class players except Gary Lineker and Bryan Robson. There was also Paul Gascoigne of course. Possessed of great natural talent 'Gazza' was a loose cannon who could transform any game in a twinkle but, equally quickly, could lose the ball – and the plot – in important positions.

The 1990 squad was by far the most experienced ever going into a World Cup, and Peter Shilton's 117 caps contributed greatly to that experience. Losing Robson in only the second game was a big blow.

'HAVE YOU EVER WITNESSED A MORE EMBARRASSING EXHIBITION OF WASTED ENERGY?' [*DAILY MAIL*]

The opening game with the Republic of Ireland was a typically British affair, with the ball spending most of the game in the air. Post-match stats show the ball in play for only 47 of the 90 minutes.

Lineker scored after eight minutes to match

Gazza cries his way home after a semi-final defeat

Hurst's achievement of scoring the last goal in a previous World Cup and the first in the next for England. The next 65 minutes of the game against the Irish was a bruising battle before a mistake by substitute Steve McMahon gifted Kevin Sheedy his equaliser.

For the Holland game, England manager Bobby Robson changed his formation to employ a sweeper for the first time in his eight-year tenure, with Mark

ENGLAND SQUAD

	CLUB	AGE	CAPS	GOALS
GOALKEEPERS				
Peter Shilton	Derby	40	117	
Chris Woods	Rangers	30	16	
David Seaman*	Arsenal	26	3	
Dave Beasant	Chelsea	31	2	
FULL BACKS				
Tony Dorigo	Cheslea	24	3	
Paul Parker	QPR	26	5	
Stuart Pearce	Notts Forest	28	23	1
Gary M Stevens	Rangers	27	38	
CENTRE BACKS				
Terry Butcher	Rangers	31	71	3
Des Walker	Notts Forest	24	17	
Mark Wright	Derby	26	23	
MIDFIELDERS				
Paul Gascoigne	Tottenham	22	10	2
Steve Hodge	Notts Forest	27	21	
Steve McMahon	Liverpool	28	12	
David Platt	Aston Villa	23	4	
Bryan Robson	Man Utd	33	84	26
Trevor Steven	Rangers	26	26	4
Neil Webb	Man Utd	26	19	2
FORWARDS				
John Barnes	Liverpool	26	52	10
Peter Beardsley	Liverpool	29	39	7
Steve Bull	Wolves	25	6	4
Gary Lineker	Tottenham	29	50	31
Chris Waddle	Marseilles	29	51	6

*After arriving in Italy David Seaman was injured in training and Dave Beasant replaced him

Previous page: BACK L-R: Waddle, Webb, Wright, Woods, Shilton, Seaman, Beasant, Steven T, Lineker, Bull, Pearce, Barnes, Butcher. FRONT L-R: Walker, Platt, McMahon, Dorigo, Parker, Stevens G, Beardsley, Gascoigne, Hodge. Robson B is missing, through injury

THE MANAGER: BOBBY ROBSON

Bobby had been a teammate of Johnny Haynes, England's first £100 a week footballer, at Fulham, before moving to West Brom where he excelled as an attacking midfielder. He won 20 England caps between 1958 and 1962 but never hit the heights of the game that he did as manager.

He returned to Craven Cottage to begin his coaching career under Ron Greenwood, and became Fulham manager in 1968 but was sacked after only nine months. He then became manager of Ipswich Town. After surviving an uncertain start to his tenure, he engineered a minor miracle and, on limited resources, turned the East Anglian club into a major football force, their success built on playing quality football on the ground.

In 1978 Ipswich won the FA Cup and at the start of the 1980s finished as First Division runners-up as well as claiming the 1981 UEFA Cup.

During his eight years in charge of England Robson took them to a World Cup quarter-final (in 1986) and a semi (in 1990), which was lost on penalties, making him the most successful England manager after Alf Ramsey. Forget about the European Championships in 1988, when England lost all three games (see page 95). He won almost half of the games that England played with him in charge, drew a third and lost only 18%.

Ultimately of course, Robson's reign will be best remembered for the team's success at Italia '90, their poorly taken penalties and what could and should have been only England's second World Cup final appearance.

ROBSON'S ENGLAND RECORD IN FULL

P	W	D	L	F	A	WIN %
95	47	30	18	154	60	49.47

STEVE BULL had never played in the Second Division let alone the First, yet Robson made him the first player to be plucked from the Third Division since Peter Taylor in 1976. In his defence 'Bully' went to Italia '90 with a goals per game ratio bettered only by Gary Lineker.

IAN WRIGHT twice broke his leg during the 1989–90 season but still scored two goals as a sub for Crystal Palace in the FA Cup Final against Man United. Despite setting a record of 27 league goals in 1989–90, he had to wait a year (and join Arsenal) before his debut.

Wright given the role. Dutch team selection wrecked that ploy and resulted in left-sided England centre half Terry Butcher playing at right back. Gascoigne dominated midfield and Des Walker had the edge over Dutch striker Marco van Basten, but the closest the match came to a goal was when England substitute Steve Bull flashed a header wide. A compelling game gave Peter Shilton a clean sheet to celebrate his world-record 120th cap and saw the elimination of Bryan Robson from the tournament with another crock; this time, fittingly, it was his Achilles heel that suffered.

Because all the group games had been draws England needed only a win over Egypt to clinch the group. And they had never lost to an African nation.

For the first time, for club or country, Robson dropped Butcher and captain Bryan Robson was unfit (despite a faith healer being flown out to aid his recuperation). England fielded a flat back four and Mark Wright, who replaced Terry Butcher, headed home the only goal of the game.

An uninspiring Second Round game with Belgium was one minute from penalties until David Platt's wonder volley, his first goal for England, set up a clash with Cameroon, the first African side to reach a World Cup quarter-final. The African team's over-physical approach had earned them two red and eight yellow cards and the suspension of four key players for the England match.

David Platt scored the 100th goal of Italia '90 to put England ahead but just past the hour Kunde and Ekeke earned Cameroon the lead. Back in London it was claimed that the celebrations in the Cameroon embassy were such that a terrorist raid was suspected and reported by neighbours.

Cameroon then attempted to sit back on their 2-1 lead rather than go for a third, of which they looked more than capable. But seven minutes from full time Lineker was felled in the box; he stood up, kept his nerve and converted England's first World Cup penalty for 20 years. In extra-time another Lineker spot kick earned England their first World Cup semi-final to be played on foreign soil.

'WE BEAT THEM IN '45, WE BEAT THEM IN '66, NOW THE BATTLE OF '90' [THE *SUN*]

England's opponents in the semi-final were the old enemy, West Germany. Since 1966 England had only beaten them twice in 10 attempts, and then both in friendly matches. England were in only their second semi-final; the Germans had reached the last four a total of eight times already.

A pulsating first half failed to create any clear-cut

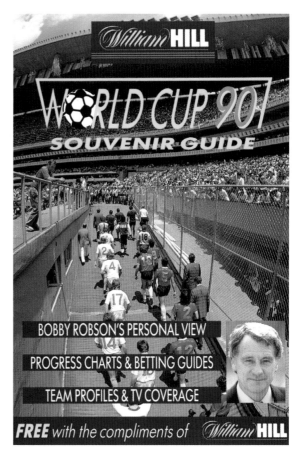

Who'd bet on England going out on penalties?

chances for either side but the Germans scored on the hour. A free kick was touched short to Brehme and his shot deflected off Parker and over Shilton. Once again Gary Lineker came to the rescue and scored his 10th World Cup goal, earning extra-time. Paul Gascoigne was later booked and realised that this, his second yellow card of the tournament, would mean that he had to miss the final. He broke down in tears on the pitch and produced the defining image of the tournament.

West Germany had dominated England in extra-time, but the English hit the post through Waddle. The

MOST DANGEROUS ENGLAND PLAYER

In 1990 there was no better goalscorer in the world than **GARY LINEKER**. Not only was he a supreme penalty box predator but his ability to keep a cool head while those around him lost theirs, as typified by his successful penalties against Cameroon, proved to be without equal. Lineker could disguise his intent when attempting to score, dummying keeper or defender or forcing them to make mistakes, which brought him 48 goals in 80 internationals. Only Bobby Charlton had scored (one) more, in 106 games.

game finished goalless and so it went to penalties.

Few supporters can remember who scored from the spot that day but everyone knows it was Pearce and Waddle who didn't. At least Psycho hit the target, with Illgner saving with his legs. Waddle's shot not only sailed over the bar, but it cleared the running track and ended up in the arms of a fan who went on to auction it on eBay, ten years later. That fan had been a hundred metres away from the spot that marked the end of yet another England World Cup dream.

England did at least return with something, though. Yes, they lost the new third place play-off game to hosts Italy 2-1, but they were awarded the FIFA Fair Play Trophy, for fewest red and yellow cards collected and fewest fouls committed.

WORLD CUP 1990 FINALS

GROUP F WINNERS: ENGLAND

England 1st P4/W1/D2/L0/F2/A1

England 1 (Lineker) v Republic of Ireland 1 (Sheedy)

11 June 1990 (Cagliari)

England 0 v Holland 0

16 June 1990 (Cagliari)

England 1 (Wright) v Egypt 0

21 June 1990 (Cagliari)

ROUND OF 16

England 1 (Platt) v Belgium 0 (AET)

26 June 1990 (Bologna)

QUARTER-FINAL

England 3 (Platt, Lineker 2 pens) v Cameroon 2 (Kunde, Ekeke) (AET)

1 July 1990 (Naples)

SEMI-FINAL

England 1 (Lineker) v West Germany 1 (Parker o.g.) (AET)
West Germany win 4-3 on penalties

4 July 1990 (Turin)

THIRD PLACE PLAY-OFF

England 1 (Platt) v Italy 2 (Baggio, Schillaci pen)

7 July 1990 (Bari)

THE FINAL

Argentina 0 v West Germany 1 (Brehme, pen)

8 July 1990 (Rome)

MAP OF VENUES

Group **A** ROME/FLORENCE
Italy, Austria, USA, Czechoslovakia

Group **B** NAPLES/BARI
Argentina, Cameroon, USSR, Romania

Group **C** TURIN/GENOVA
Brazil, Sweden, Costa Rica, Scotland

Group **D** MILAN/BOLOGNA
W. Germany, Yugoslavia, UAE, Colombia

Group **E** VERONA/UDINE
Belgium, S. Korea, Uruguay, Spain

Group **F** CAGLIARI/PALERMO
England, Eire, Holland, Egypt

MATCH DATES

JUNE 11		
Group C	COSTA RICA v SCOTLAND	Genoa at 4.00pm BST
Group E	ENGLAND v EIRE	Cagliari at 8.00pm BST
JUNE 16		
Group C	SWEDEN v SCOTLAND	Genoa at 8.00pm BST
Group F	ENGLAND v HOLLAND	Cagliari at 8.00pm BST
JUNE 17		
Group F	EIRE v EGYPT	Palermo at 4.00pm BST
JUNE 20		
Group C	BRAZIL v SCOTLAND	Turin at 8.00pm BST
JUNE 21		
Group F	ENGLAND v EGYPT	Cagliari at 8.00pm BST
Group F	EIRE V HOLLAND	Palermo at 8.00pm BST

A very useful guide to who, where and when at Italia '90

ENGLAND'S WORST EVER TEAM

There are so many candidates for this team, but the choice of captain encapsulates all that has been so wrong with the English national team. Carlton Palmer's career trophies number 0, but his transfer sums add up to £6 million. As manager of Stockport County he asked, 'Who is to say I won't be manager of England in 10 years time?' They were relegated after a record 32 defeats.

GLEN JOHNSON ('03–'05, CAPS 5)

West Ham ('01–'03), Chelsea ('03–), Portsmouth ('06–'07 loan)

After only 15 games for West Ham (and eight at Millwall on loan), was transferred to Chelsea for loads of dosh. Capped by Sven for two starts, got two yellow cards and impressed no-one in any of the friendlies he played. Loaned out by Chelsea and not recalled despite injury problems in 2006–7.

GRAHAM ROBERTS ('83–'84, CAPS 6)

Weymouth ('78–'80), Spurs ('80–'87), Rangers ('87–'88), Chelsea ('88–'90), WBA ('90–'92)

Won Cups with Spurs and Rangers. Games for England included just two wins (one v Scotland, one v N. Ireland), two draws (same opposition) and two losses, both friendlies (0-2 to France, 0-2 to USSR), all for Bobby Robson.

TONY TOWERS ('76, CAPS 3)

Man City ('69–'74), Sunderland ('74–'77), Birmingham ('77–'81)

Was a makeweight in the deal which took Dennis Tueart and Mick Horswill to Man City for £275,000 from Sunderland. Played for England against Wales (won 1-0), N. Ireland (on as a sub for 23 minutes in a 4-0 win) and Italy (a 3-2 win in the US Bicentennial Tournament, in New York). But why?

PAUL STEWART ('91–'92, CAPS 3)

Blackpool ('81–'87), Man City ('87–'88), Spurs ('88–'92), Liverpool ('92–'96), Crystal Palace ('94 loan), Wolves ('94 loan), Burnley ('95 loan), Sunderland ('95 loan, '96–'97), Stoke ('97–'98)

Total playing time for England 78 minutes, one loss (to Germany), two draws. Always confident of his own abilities, none of his 10 managers could see his true brilliance.

SUBS

GK Dave Beasant ('89, caps 2)
Broke his foot with a jar of mayonnaise, his nickname was Lurch.

Mike Duxbury ('83–'84, caps 10)
At Man Utd he won two FA Cups. Because he was at Man Utd.

Bob McNab ('68–'69, caps 4)
Now best known as the father of Mercedes McNab, a co-star of Buffy the Vampire Slayer.

Brian Deane ('91–'92, caps 3)
Scored seven goals in 18 games for Benfica, apparently.

GARRY BIRTLES ('80, CAPS 3)

Notts Forest ('76–'80, '82–'87), Man Utd ('80–'82), Notts County ('87–'88), Grimsby Town ('88–'91)

Cost Man Utd £1.25 million. Didn't score for England, but didn't finish a game, either. Played 15 mins as sub in a 3-1 friendly win against Argentina, 75 mins against Italy in 1-0 loss, and 65 mins in a 2-1 loss to the Czechs. Had a beard.

GK: RICHARD WRIGHT ('00–'01, CAPS 2)

Ipswich Town ('94–'01), Arsenal ('01–'02), Everton ('02–)

Cost Arsenal £6 million and played only 12 games (1 o.g.). At Everton, he fell out of his loft and in 2006 injured himself warming up. First cap in a 2-1 friendly win away to Malta, 2nd as half-time sub for Nigel Martyn in friendly loss to Holland at White Hart Lane. Been in 30 England squads.

STEVE FOSTER ('82, CAPS 3)

Portsmouth ('75–'79), Brighton & Hove Albion ('79–'84, '92–'96), Aston Villa ('84), Luton Town ('84–'89), Oxford Utd ('89–'92)

Famous for always wearing a fluffy white tennis headband, won the League Cup with Luton in 1989. England didn't concede in any of his three games, but they were against N. Ireland, Kuwait and Holland starring no-one you'd recall.

PAUL KONCHESKY ('03-'05, CAPS 2)

Charlton Athletic ('99–'05), West Ham ('05–)

Sven capped an enormous number of players, some of whom deserved a chance. Konchesky however, didn't. With Ashley Cole and Wayne Bridge as first-choice left backs Sven still tried him out for 45 mins against Australia (lost 1-3) and 45 v Argentina (won 3-2). Unlikely to ever gain another cap.

CARLTON PALMER ('92–'93, CAPS 18, 1 GOAL)

WBA ('84–'89), Sheff Wed ('89–'94, '01 loan), Leeds Utd ('94–'97), Saints ('97–'99), Notts Forest ('99), Coventry ('99–'01), Watford ('00–'01 loan), Stockport County ('01–'03), Mansfield ('05)

Not a misprint. Carlton has 18 caps. And he scored in a World Cup qualifier (a 6-0 win over San Marino at Wembley). Often preferred to Steve Bruce. Why? Ask the turnip.

ERIC GATES ('80, CAPS 2)

Ipswich Town ('73–'85), Sunderland ('85–'90), Carlisle ('90–'91)

Under Bobby Robson at Ipswich Eric Lazenby Gates scored 96 goals in 345 games and won the 1978 FA Cup and the 1981 UEFA Cup. But it was Greenwood who gave him his two caps. Unfortunately, the second was only for the first half of a World Cup qualifier that England lost 2-1 in Bucharest.

JOHN FASHANU ('89, CAPS 2)

Norwich ('79–'83), Crystal Palace ('83 loan), Lincoln City ('83–'84), Millwall ('84–'86), Wimbledon ('86–'94), Aston Villa ('94)

Was involved in a match-fixing scandal and retired to work in TV (*Gladiators*) in 1995. Both caps came in a friendly tournament at Wembley. Played 71 mins in a 0-0 with Chile, and 31 mins in a 2-0 win over Scotland (replaced by Steve Bull).

MANAGER: HOWARD WILKINSON

Managed Notts County ('82–'83), Sheff Wed ('83–'88), Leeds Utd ('88–'96), Sunderland ('02–'03)

As a club manager he won the Second and First Division titles, both with Leeds and er, that's it. Took temporary charge of the England squad after the sacking of Glenn Hoddle and lost 2-0 to France. Took charge of the national team again after Keegan's departure, for a 0-0 with Finland. Managed Sunderland to their record run of 19 defeats in the Premiership and was sacked (they were relegated).

Wilkinson's England record: P2/W0/D1/L1/F0/A2

EUROPEAN
CHAMPIONSHIPS SWEDEN 1992

'FOR GOD'S SAKE, GO!' [THE WHOLE ENGLISH NATION]

The amazing story of Euro '92 was that after the first round of games, the tabloids went for the England manager's throat in a manner in which they had never gone for a manager before. Headlines were insulting, derogatory and very funny.

The other story of the Championships was that the eventual winners, Denmark, hadn't actually qualified for the finals. Because Yugoslavia, who had won their qualifying group, was being torn apart by civil war at the time, UEFA decided to punish the national football team (well, they couldn't capture Milosevic, could they?). They kicked the Yugoslavs out and Denmark, who had finished runners-up in their qualifying group, were given the slot. With just 11 days' notice, Denmark arrived to face one of the favourites for Group 1 in their first game. Yes, despite England having won only half their qualifying games against the footballing might of Northern Ireland, Turkey and Poland (drawing the rest), they were over-optimistically considered obvious winners – or at least certain to progress to the semi-finals. And this despite the fact that the England team who arrived in Malmo for their first game was missing the mercurial talent of Paul Gascoigne (still not recovered from his flying tackle on Notts Forest's Gary Charles in the 1991 FA Cup final). But it was OK because they had… Carlton Palmer.

Manager Graham Taylor had taken over from Bobby Robson in the wake of England's fine showing at Italia '90. He had one warm-up friendly game (they beat Hungary 1-0 at Wembley) before being plunged straight into the Euro qualifiers. A competent club coach who'd only managed Watford and Aston Villa, Taylor was not prepared for or able to cope with the level of press and public opprobrium that would be heaped upon him during his reign as England manager. A fan of the 'Route 1' to goal philosophy (so beloved of Howard Wilkinson), his club teams had been fine exponents of

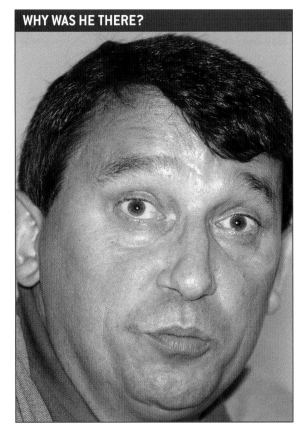

WHY WAS HE THERE?

the art. Unfortunately, his international players were more used to attempting to pass the ball towards goal instead of hoofing it high, and so he brought in some less skilful players who were able and willing to 'go direct'. Not that it worked, as their lack of goals in qualifying testified – seven in six games was to prove average for England as managed by Taylor. His career total as international manager was 1.6 goals per game, compared with 1.9 for Sir Alf, 1.85 for Ron Greenwood and 1.9 for Sven.

And so, despite the Danes' lack of preparation for the Euros, were it not for the width of a post John Jensen, soon to achieve legendary status at Highbury for his profligacy in an Arsenal shirt, would have given

ENGLAND SQUAD

	CLUB	AGE	CAPS	GOALS
GOALKEEPERS				
Chris Woods	Sheff Wed	32	31	
Nigel Martyn	Crystal Palace	25	2	
FULL BACKS				
Stuart Pearce	Notts Forest	30	47	2
Tony Dorigo	Leeds	26	10	
CENTRE BACKS				
Keith Curle	Man City	28	2	
Martin Keown	Everton	25	6	1
Des Walker	Notts Forest	26	44	
Mark Wright	Liverpool	28	42	1
MIDFIELD				
David Platt	Bari	26	29	10
Trevor Steven	Marseilles	28	34	4
Nigel Clough	Notts Forest	26	7	
Andy Sinton	QPR	26	4	
Carlton Palmer	Sheff Wed	26	4	
Neil Webb	Man Utd	28	24	4
Tony Daley	Aston Villa	24	5	
David Batty	Leeds	23	8	
FORWARDS				
Gary Lineker	Tottenham	31	77	48
Paul Merson	Arsenal	24	5	1
Alan Smith	Arsenal	29	11	2
Alan Shearer	S'hampton	21	2	1

Previous page: BACK L-R: Curle, Smith, Palmer, Lineker, Woods. FRONT L-R: Merson, Platt, Walker, Steven, Pearce. The man on the left end and not in the photo was Martin Keown. Nice shot of the marching band though, eh? Before their opening game against Denmark, which finished 0-0.

THE MANAGER: GRAHAM TAYLOR

Graham Taylor was yet another successful club manager who never cut it in the England job. After becoming the youngest FA Coach at 27, he became the youngest manager in the country a year later when he took over at Lincoln City, the second club he'd played for, after Grimsby.

He won the first of five promotions in club management when he steered The Imps to the Fourth Division title in 1976. He moved to Vicarage Road and five years later Watford had climbed from Division Four to the top flight. In 1983 they were runners-up in the title race and a year later lost the FA Cup final to Everton.

Taylor then got his biggest career break when Aston Villa offered him the manager's job in 1987 and he led them back into the First Division. He achieved 2nd spot in the First division before becoming England manager. Which says a lot.

As an average Fourth Division defender, Taylor had no top-flight experience of playing the game. So he replaced England coach Don Howe with Steve Harrison, who was similarly deficient in top-level experience.

It was to bother Taylor throughout his managerial career that he had trouble eliciting respect from top players because he hadn't been one himself. He made Gary Lineker captain, instead of natural leaders Bryan Robson or Terry Butcher, but began his reign on the field well enough, going through 1990 unbeaten in all three games. In getting to Sweden England lost just once in 18 games, to Germany (of course). In case anyone got any strange ideas about England winning another trophy though, they were dumped out of Euro '92 bottom of their four-team group, having scored just a single goal. Taylor would no doubt point to the fact that they only conceded two as a positive sign.

TAYLOR'S ENGLAND RECORD 12 SEPT 1990 – 17 JUNE 1992						
P	W	D	L	F	A	WIN%
24	13	9	2	34	17	54.6

them a winning start. Tony Daley got himself sent off for England who managed to huff and puff their way to a goalless draw.

France, the other favourites to progress from the group, were up next. They had also drawn their opening fixture against Sweden, 1-1. They blatantly played for a draw against England (the cunning swines), and helped to produce a game of startling mediocrity. Stuart Pearce, after being headbutted by Boli, almost exacted the best kind of retribution but his thunderous free-kick hit the bar. Even the late introduction of Alan Shearer failed to produce a goal. France wouldn't qualify for the semis either, though.

SWEDES 2 TURNIPS 1 *(THE SUN)*

Two games, two draws and no goals left England needing to beat Sweden to reach the semi-finals and when David Platt, the best goal-getting midfielder Villa had seen for a long time, netted a volley after just three minutes it looked possible. Andy Sinton (remember him?) and Tony Daley then had chances to increase the lead but failed. Jan Eriksson headed an equaliser for Sweden early in the second half. Thomas Brolin – he was fat, he was round, but he certainly got around – scored the winner eight minutes from time and England were out, and bottom of the group (France had the same points and goal difference, but had scored one more than England managed).

Graham Taylor naturally bore the brunt of the abuse from supporters and media alike. Deservedly so. Taylor changed the England formation three times in the three group games from a back four to a sweeper system and back again. Gary Lineker had three different strike partners (Alan Shearer, Alan Smith and David Platt), but little back-up from 'flair' players.

Taylor took just two recognised full backs, both left footers, to Sweden. Injury robbed him of Rob Jones, Gary Stevens and Lee Dixon so he made-do with Keith

WHY WASN'T HE THERE?

Although he was part of the squad, **NIGEL CLOUGH** never got a kick in Sweden, yet players with less ability, guile and football acumen were capped. Palmer and Sinton were just two of the midfielders who couldn't hold a candle to young Cloughie, who was one of the best passers in the country. Using him may have prised a few openings in the three games England played to produce just a single goal. He was also likely to come up with a goal or two himself.

Curle (normally a centre back) against Denmark and David Batty (a midfielder) against France and Sweden. Perhaps more amazingly though, Taylor kept that renowned international footballer Carlton Palmer in the midfield for every game.

Gary Lineker went to Sweden with 48 goals to his name, just one short of Bobby Charlton's international record, but failed to score. Taylor ignominiously substituted his captain and chief goalscorer in the 64th minute against Sweden, replacing him with Alan Smith. Maybe Taylor blamed Lineker and was trying to deflect some of the adverse reaction from fans and media away from himself onto Lineker. It didn't work. Everyone wondered why he'd withdrawn one of the international game's greatest goal poachers when the team desperately needed to score.

MOST DANGEROUS ENGLAND PLAYER

DAVID PLATT, if only by default, since he managed to score the only goal England registered in Sweden. In truth there wasn't really a dangerous England player at what was England's worst tournament performance ever. Unless you count most dangerous to England themselves, in which case it would be any of the other seven midfield players, none of whom were capable of controlling a game or of making a telling forward pass to Lineker or Shearer.

MOST DANGEROUS OPPONENT

PETER SCHMEICHEL. After denying a shot-shy England attack in the opening game the Great Dane distinguished himself in a semi-final 'shoot-out' victory over holders Holland and was awesome in the 2-0 defeat of Germany in the final.

MOST OVERRATED ENGLAND PLAYER

TONY DALEY was a skilful winger who could create goals and score them but he could also drift in and out of games to the detriment of his team. On his day he was a match winner but in one start against Sweden and one substitute appearance (against Denmark) he failed to influence the pattern of play.

EUROPEAN CHAMPIONSHIPS 1992 QUALIFYING

GROUP 7 WINNERS: ENGLAND

England P6/W3/D3/L0/F7/A3

England 2 [Lineker, Beardsley] v Poland 0

17 Oct 1990 (Wembley)

Rep Ireland 1 [Cascarino] v England 1 [Platt]

14 Nov 1990 (Dublin)

England 1 [Dixon] v Rep Ireland 1 [Quinn]

27 March 1991 (Wembley)

Turkey 0 v England 1 [Wise]

1 May 1991 (Izmir)

England 1 [Smith] v Turkey 0

16 Oct 1991 (Wembley)

Poland 1 [Szewczyk] v England 1 [Lineker]

13 Nov 1991 (Poznan)

EUROPEAN CHAMPIONSHIPS 1992 FINALS

GROUP A WINNERS: SWEDEN. DENMARK ALSO PROGRESSED

England 4th P3/W0/D2/L1/F1/A2 (eliminated)

England 0 v Denmark 0

11 June 1992 (Malmo)

England 0 v France 0

14 June 1992 (Malmo)

Sweden 2 [Eriksson, Brolin] v England [Platt] 1

17 June 1992 (Stockholm)

THE FINAL

Denmark 2 [Jensen, Vilfort] v Germany 0

26 June 1992 (Gothenborg)

WORLD CUP UNITED STATES OF AMERICA 1994

Italia '90 proved to be a watershed for English football. The rise of Ecstasy as the drug of choice for football hooligans had seen the demise of hooliganism on the terraces in the late 1980s, while the implementation of all-seater stadia had done for the rest (at least during games). The launch of Sky Sports and the beginnings of the formation of the Premier League revolutionised how football was screened on television, with the result that hordes of men and women had joined together to watch England's matches in pubs and clubs across the country as Robson's team progressed to the semi-finals and came so close to reaching another final. Gazza's tears and the drama of the penalty shoot-out added appeal to the non-fanatical watchers in England.

There was a new-found and rediscovered interest in football in England at the beginning of the new decade, thanks to the cleaning up of grounds (no more pissing into the pockets of another man's coat just because they were standing in front on the terraces) and the screening of more live games on publicly accessible screens. Graham Taylor almost blew all of it, though.

England had performed so abjectly in the European Championships of 1992 (winning no games) that he had been vilified in the tabloids as a turnip (see page 110). The press had transposed his face onto a picture of a turnip, and suggested that he seemed to have the footballing nous of a root vegetable. He could put the new-found footy fans off the game playing like that.

His response? He still had Stuart Pearce, David Platt, Des Walker and Paul Gascoigne to call upon but not wide men Barnes and Waddle, so he chose to rely on the muscle of an Ince/Batty midfield. Gary Lineker's retirement was offset by the arrival of Ian Wright and Alan Shearer. And there was always Carlton Palmer.

Holland's Ronald Koeman was at the 1994 World Cup. England weren't

RETURN OF THE TURNIP

Things didn't begin well for Taylor and his men when Norway earned a draw at Wembley in October 1992, in the first qualifying game for the 1994 World Cup. A 4-0 defeat of Turkey and 6-0 win over San Marino at Wembley (a team of bakers, butchers and whose

PLAYERS USED BY ENGLAND DURING QUALIFYING GROUP GAMES

GOALKEEPERS

Chris Woods (Sheff Wed), David Seaman (Arsenal)

FULL BACKS

Lee Dixon (Arsenal), Stuart Pearce (Notts Forest), Tony Dorigo (Leeds), David Bardsley (QPR), Rob Jones (Liverpool), Paul Parker (Man Utd)

CENTRE BACKS

Gary Pallister (Man Utd), Tony Adams (Arsenal), Des Walker (Notts Forest), Martin Keown (Arsenal)

MIDFIELDERS

Carlton Palmer (Sheff Wed), David Batty (Leeds), David Platt (Juventus), Paul Gascoigne (Lazio), Paul Ince (Man Utd), Nigel Clough (Notts Forest), Andy Sinton (QPR), Lee Sharpe (Man Utd), Stuart Ripley (Blackburn Rovers)

FORWARDS

Teddy Sheringham (Tottenham), Alan Shearer (Blackburn Rovers), Ian Wright (Arsenal), Paul Merson (Arsenal), Les Ferdinand (QPR), John Barnes (Liverpool)

THE MANAGER: GRAHAM TAYLOR

As the son of a journalist, Taylor thought he knew how to handle the media but even Goebbels couldn't have handled his hounding by the press any better. Managers are judged by results not their affability though, and had he taken the team to the World Cup finals he'd have had at least another seven months in the job before watching his team implode in America, as they undoubtedly would have done. They won five games in 14 months of qualifying and although they scored 28 goals, almost half of those came against San Marino.

If future England teams could learn anything from Taylor's tenure it was that in international football Route One didn't always work – he insisted on players getting the ball forward as quickly as possible and playing off a big centre forward. Taylor, like Revie, Greenwood and Robson before him, had built club success by cultivating a tightly knit, family unit. That cannot be done in international football.

Finally, Taylor should never have agreed to allow TV cameras to record everything said in training and during games. Mind you, it did give us the peculiar catchphrase, 'Do I not like that.'

His language was as confused as his tactics.

TAYLOR'S ENGLAND RECORD 9 SEPT 1992 – 17 NOV 1993						
P	W	D	L	F	A	WIN%
14	5	4	5	28	15	35.7

goalkeeper Benedettini was a travel agent who drove the team bus), followed for England.

At the end of April 1993 England faced a Dutch team who knew that if they lost the game at Wembley they wouldn't go to the 1994 finals. Graham Taylor felt the Dutch were weak in defence and so picked an attacking team. After 20 minutes England led 2-0, through Barnes and Platt. And then Dennis Bergkamp scored and with four minutes remaining Des Walker pulled Marc Overmars back to concede a penalty which van Vossen converted to earn a draw. A month later Teddy Sheringham made his debut as England struggled to a 1-1 draw in Poland, with sub Ian Wright scoring an 84th-minute equaliser.

On 2 June 1993 Norway tore England apart in Oslo. Graham Taylor selected a trio of tall defenders (Pallister, Walker, Adams) to combat the 6' 4" aerial threat of Jostein Flo. It worked and Flo didn't score. Unfortunately, both Leonhardsen and Bohinen did though, and the second was the 400th goal conceded by England. It was their first defeat in a World Cup qualifier since losing to Norway in 1981 and meant that England

CARLTON PALMER. Do I not like that. Above, Carlton receives the captain's armband from Gary Lineker, who is leaving the field for the last time as an England international. Carlton went on to play 11 more times for England after this game, including every one of the qualifiers for this 1994 World Cup in the USA. Exactly why Palmer, who was a middling, athletic, tough-tackling ball winner with Sheffield Wednesday, should have been elevated to such an exalted position can only be because he would willingly play to manager Taylor's game plan without question.

GARY LINEKER. He was 29 when Taylor substituted him so ignominiously in Sweden (above) in 1992 and, despite suffering a toe injury in Japan, he managed to play 17 games at the end of the 1993–'94 season and score six goals. An international superstar, he would have added a presence to any England squad and if Taylor hadn't been such a turnip, Lineker could have contributed some sorely lacking calm assessment of what was actually happening in games. As the documentary *Do I Not Like That* showed, there was clearly no-one else in the England team capable of that.

had to win all three of their remaining qualifiers to reach the finals. They beat Poland at Wembley in September 1993 and then travelled to Rotterdam to face the Dutch, on 13 October 1993.

It was all going so well for England when David Platt tore into the Dutch penalty area only to be hauled back, blatantly, by Ronald Koeman after an hour's goalless

play. But a free-kick just outside the area was awarded and the home skipper was not dismissed, as he later agreed he should have been. Two minutes later, instead of sitting in an early bath, Koeman was celebrating his stunning free-kick goal. Bergkamp added a second six minutes later and, as television sound mikes clearly picked up, Graham Taylor commented to the fourth

MOST DANGEROUS ENGLAND PLAYER

DAVID PLATT. Paul Gascoigne was back to his best, although suspended for the Holland game, but Platt was a one-man scoring machine. He took a record of nine goals in his previous 11 games into the match in Rotterdam and, but for Koeman, might have added at least one to that tally.

MOST DANGEROUS OPPONENT

KARL-JOSEF ASSENMACHER. At the risk of sounding like Jose Mourinho, the referee of the second game against Holland cost England the game and qualification to the finals, and in doing that cost the FA millions of pounds in revenue from TV and sponsorship. Ronald Koeman should have been sent off for his professional foul on Platt and a penalty awarded to England. (Not that they would have scored, of course.)

WORLD CUP 1994 QUALIFYING

GROUP 2 WINNERS: NORWAY. HOLLAND ALSO QUALIFIED
England 3rd P10/W5/D2/L2/F26/A9 did not qualify
England 1 [Platt] v Norway 1 [Rekdal]
14 Oct 1992 (Wembley)
England 4 [Gascoigne (2), Pearce, Shearer] v Turkey 0
18 Nov 1992 (Wembley)
England 6 [Platt (4), Palmer, Ferdinand] v San Marino 0
17 Feb 1993 (Wembley)
Turkey 0 v England 2 [Platt, Gascoigne]
31 March 1993 (Izmir)
England 2 [Barnes, Platt] v Holland 2 [Bergkamp, Van Vossen]
28 April 1993 (Wembley)
Poland 1 [Adamczuk] v England 1 [Wright]
29 May 1993 (Chorzow)
Norway 2 [Leonhardsen, Bohinen] v England 0
2 June 1993 (Oslo)
England 3 [Ferdinand, Gascoigne, Pearce] v Poland 0
8 Sept 1993 (Wembley)
Holland 2 [Koeman, Bergkamp] v England 0
13 Oct 1993 (Rotterdam)
England 7 [Ince (2), Wright (4), Ferdinand] v San Marino 1 [Gualtieri]
17 Nov 1993 (Wembley)

THE FINAL
Brazil 0 v Italy 0 (AET)
Brazil won 3-2 in a penalty shoot-out
17 July 1994 (Pasadena)

official, after Koeman's trip on Platt, 'Thank you very much, you have just cost me my job.'

But the Dutch result wasn't exactly what cost Taylor his job. That would be down to Stuart Pearce in the final, meaningless qualifier to be played against San Marino in Bologna, Italy, when he under-hit a pass back to Seaman after seven seconds of play. Davide Gualtieri (not related to the Argentinian General who led the failed assault on the Falklands - yes, yes, I know it's spelt differently) nipped in and scored one of the fastest goals in international football. England recovered and scored seven themselves, but the fact remained that, as in 1974 and 1978, England had no World Cup to look forward to.

Taylor's resignation was demanded again by the media and this time he did go.

The Dutch finally went out to Brazil in the quarter-finals, 2-3 in the USA, but Norway came bottom of their group, with Mexico and Rep. Ireland going through with Italy who were third in that group! Italy then scraped into the quarter-finals, coming fourth in the group of six

playing the third-place play-offs. They then beat Nigeria (AET), Spain and Bulgaria to reach the final, which they lost on penalties to Brazil after a 0-0 bore draw.

I tell you all this because it's highly unlikely that you remember that there was a World Cup in 1994. I do not assume that you care.

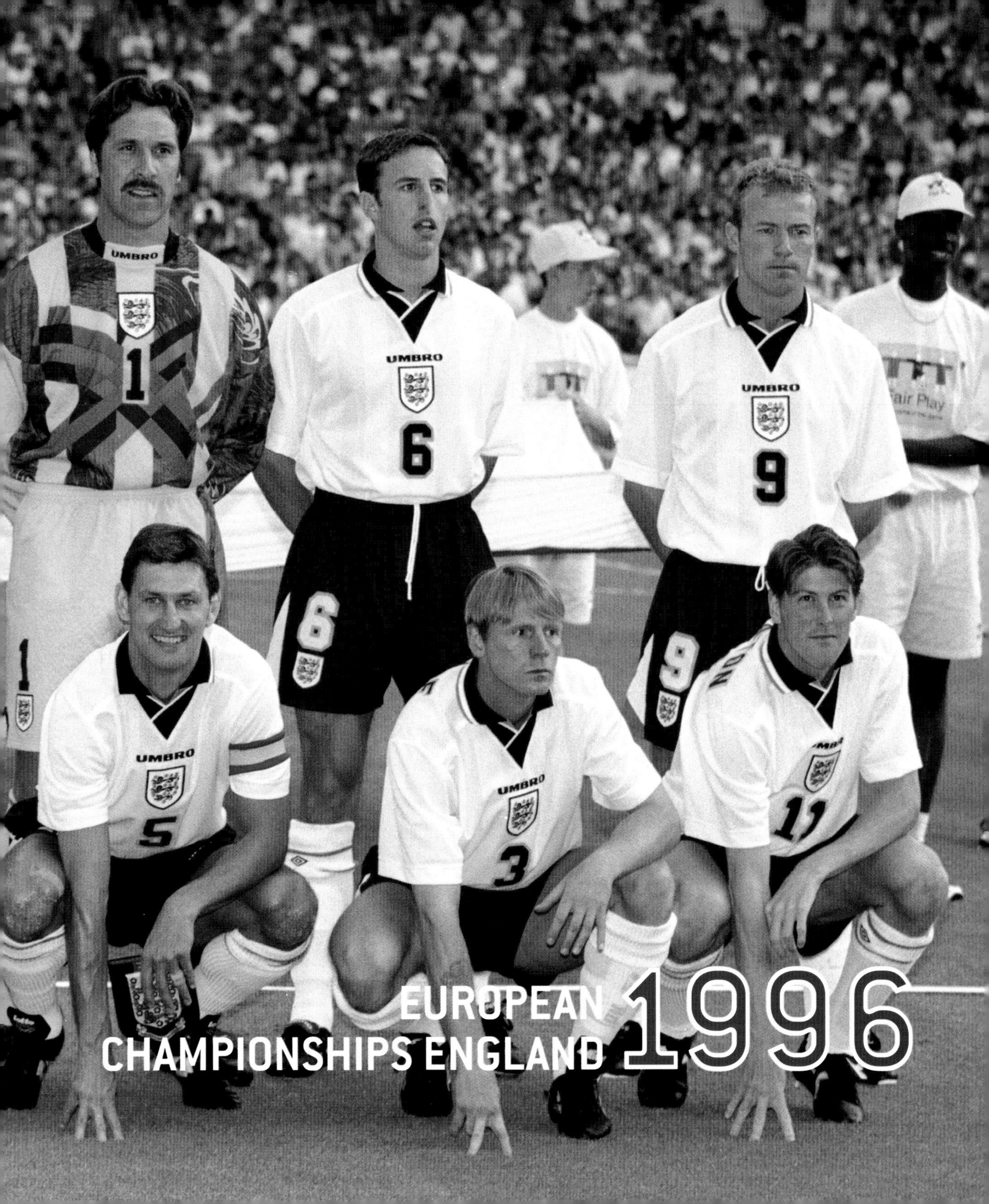

EUROPEAN CHAMPIONSHIPS ENGLAND 1996

'FOOTBALL'S COMING HOME' (BADDIEL & SKINNER)

The expectation that England had lived with for 30 years was finally about to be fulfilled with Euro '96. Or so we were informed by excessive media hype, and the chorus of that irritating chart hit by those irritating comedians Baddiel and Skinner. 'Football's Coming Home' became the competition's anthem.

Depending on what you read, listened to or watched at the time, the country was split between those who believed that England merely had to turn up to win, and those who were completely apathetic about the event.

Everyone proclaimed home advantage was the crucial factor in 1996 as it had been 30 years earlier. Coach Terry Venables (because of his recent non-football business problems, the FA didn't want his title to be manager) had the pick of some outstanding, if somewhat unpredictable, football talent.

Excitingly, the build-up to the tournament had been blighted by misbehaviour by those players on a pre-tournament tour of the Far East. There were widely reported stories of drinking games in Hong Kong nightclubs (in 'the dentist's chair') and of alcohol-induced misbehaviour by players on the flight home. The squad closed ranks and Venables, while promising action against any guilty player, warned the press against making Gazza the scapegoat – despite the pictorial evidence of Gascoigne in 'the dentist's chair', proving his involvement, along with Teddy Sheringham.

FOOTBALL LEGENDS
DUNCAN EDWARDS 1936–1958

The Neville brothers were the first siblings to play for England at the same time since the Charltons: smaller than a postage stamp, but hard-tackling

ENGLAND SQUAD

	TEAM	AGE	CAPS	GOALS
GOALKEEPERS				
David Seaman	Arsenal	32	24	
Tim Flowers	Blackburn	29	8	
Ian Walker	Tottenham	24	2	
DEFENDERS				
Gary Neville	Man Utd	21	10	
Sol Campbell	Tottenham	19	1	
Tony Adams	Arsenal	29	40	4
Gareth Southgate	Aston Villa	25	4	
Stuart Pearce	Notts Forest	34	65	5
Steve Howey	Newcastle	24	4	
MIDFIELD				
Steve McManaman	Liverpool	24	10	
Paul Gascoigne	Rangers	29	38	7
David Platt	Arsenal	29	58	27
Steve Stone	Notts Forest	24	6	2
Paul Ince	Inter Milan	28	19	2
Phil Neville	Man Utd	19	1	
Jamie Redknapp	Liverpool	22	4	
Darren Anderton	Tottenham	24	11	5
Nicky Barmby	Middlesbro'	21	6	2
FORWARDS				
Teddy Sheringham	Tottenham	30	15	2
Alan Shearer	Blackburn	25	23	5
Les Ferdinand	Newcastle	29	10	4
Robbie Fowler	Liverpool	21	3	

Previous page: BACK L-R: Ince, McManaman, Seaman, Southgate, Shearer. FRONT L-R: Neville G, Gascoigne, Sheringham, Adams, Pearce, Anderton line up before trouncing Holland 4-1 at Wembley

THE MANAGER: TERRY VENABLES

No England manager had ever taken so much excess baggage into the job and no England coach has ever been so widely respected. The first player to represent England at all levels, from schoolboy to the senior side, Venables was no run-of-the mill footballer and after playing for Chelsea joined Spurs in 1966 before winning the FA Cup the following year in the first ever all-London final against his former club. He began his coaching career with QPR and Crystal Palace and then took QPR to the 1982 FA Cup final before going to Barcelona in 1984 where he steered them to their first La Liga title for 11 years. Twelve months later Barça lost the European Cup Final and in 1987 he was sacked before heading home as manager of Spurs.

He won the 1991 FA Cup and left in 1993. He then became England manager. When the FA appointed him as coach they inserted an escape clause in his contract because of business dealings which were the subject of a BBC *Panorama* programme (with another pending).

Venables recalled Don Howe and brought Bryan Robson in to the management team and set about preparing for Euro '96. His preparations were not enough, of course, and before the tournament ended his successor had been appointed.

Venables left as press pressure came to bear on him, but what would the FA have done if Gareth Southgate had not missed and England had gone on to win the trophy?

VENABLES' ENGLAND RECORD 9 MARCH 1994 – 26 JUNE 1996

P	W	D	L	F	A	WIN%
24	11	11	2	35	14	47.82

STEVE STONE. A very English-style winger, built for speed like a Dagenham fast Ford, he was an ineffective sub in three of England's games at the finals, two of which were draws.

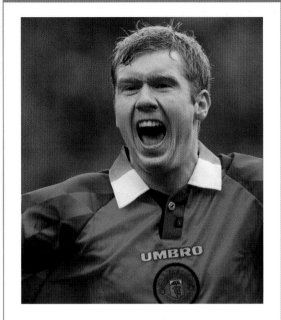

PAUL SCHOLES. A year later he scored against Italy in only his second game, and had scored 13 goals in Utd's title-winning team of 1995–96. He could have changed games as a sub.

The England players accepted collective responsibility for damage caused to their Cathay Pacific aeroplane.

It was widely believed, by those who cared, that Shearer's finishing, prompted by the technical wizardry of Paul Gascoigne and the football brain of the nearest thing we had to an old-fashioned inside-forward, Teddy Sheringham, would see us through. As would the 'they shall not pass' defensive philosophy of Tony Adams and Stuart Pearce. Then there was the persistent rumour that Steve McManaman, on his day, was the best top-flight footballer for running at the opposition, with the ball at his feet. Sadly, the proof was never found that this was the case. Still, all the England games were going to be played at Wembley. If only beer were 2/.

'THIRTY YEARS OF HURT' (IAN BROUDIE)

Shearer led the attack in the opening game against Switzerland and justified his coach's faith in him by scoring his first international goal for two years midway through the first half. Cross of St George flags were waved and collective sighs of relief were exhaled as England dominated the first half without scoring again. Unfortunately, the Swiss were not about to roll over for the hosts and seven minutes from time grabbed a penalty equaliser courtesy of Turkyilmaz.

That stalemate set up game number two quite nicely. The oldest international rivalry in the world was set for renewal. Scotland, 80-1 outsiders in what was their first European Championships, had held Holland

0-0 in their opener, so a win for either side would almost certainly guarantee progress.

England were unchanged for the game which attracted the highest attendance of the tournament, 76,864. In a pulsating first half of few chances the Scots enjoyed territorial supremacy but the half-time substitution of Jamie Redknapp for Stuart Pearce gave midfield a new direction and allowed Gascoigne the freedom to inflict his talent on the country where he then plied his trade, for Rangers. Steve McManaman switched from left to right flank and ran relentlessly at Scotland's back line. Finally, one of his passes was successful and released the overlapping Gary Neville, whose subsequent cross was meat and drink to Shearer, who headed England ahead early in the second period. (He then had a nice glass of brandy.)

The turning point of the game came 14 minutes from time. Tony Adams slid in on Gordon Durie and a penalty was given, despite everyone knowing that the striker fell over more easily than a one-legged wrestler. Up stepped Gary McAllister but Seaman saved his weak

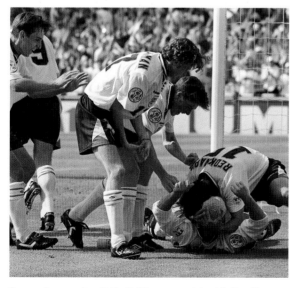

Gazza gets a snog from Teddy. But they were not drunk in Hong Kong

shot, turning the ball away for a corner. The Arsenal man collected the kick, threw out to start an attack and a couple of passes later came the goal that was eventually voted the best ever scored at Wembley.

Gascoigne chased the bouncing ball, on the right of Scotland's midfield. Colin Hendry raced in Gazza's direction to challenge him. Collision was inevitable, but somehow Gascoigne flicked the ball over Hendry's lunge with his left foot before hitting a splendid volley past Goram with his right. Game over. Gazza threw himself down beside the goal and received a dousing of water from Sheringham in imitation of the now infamous photo of the pair at play in that Chinese nightclub, closely followed by a snog.

After the match Gazza received a front-page apology from the *Daily Mirror* for all the derogatory things they had printed about him. He also took home the gratitude of a watching nation.

England then prepared to face favourites Holland, who had also won their second game 2-0, against Switzerland. The game was hailed as one of the best in England's history. Not so much for the scoreline, emphatic as 4-1 was, but for the manner in which the team dispatched one of the best football nations in the world. England were also helped in their task by apparent disharmony in the Dutch camp, where cliques had formed and player-power was being flaunted at the manager, Guus Hiddink. The little orange devils didn't like his tactics, apparently.

An unchanged England team dominated the first half and led at the interval through a Shearer penalty. Six minutes after the restart Sheringham headed home a Gascoigne corner. Next came the goal that produced an unassailable lead, and is widely agreed to be one of the best England have ever scored.

McManaman, Gascoigne and Sheringham combined for Teddy to unselfishly lay the ball off to Shearer, racing up in support, and the centre forward

MOST DANGEROUS ENGLAND PLAYER

ALAN SHEARER. He was mobile, brave and equipped with the necessary striker instincts to score any kind of goal with feet or head. Despite suffering a two-year international goal drought going into the competition, he said in a press conference before it started that 'My lack of goals for England seems to worry everyone else but it doesn't worry me.' Thankfully Terry Venables knew football better than the media pundits and stuck with his man who went on to score in every game, bar the 0-0 with Spain, of course (although he did net during the penalty shoot-out), and finished top scorer of the tournament.

MOST OVERRATED ENGLAND PLAYER

STEVE MCMANAMAN. In seven years of England selection he played 37 times and scored three goals. He was chosen by Pelé as the player of the '96 tournament and that always means he was crap. Pelé now advertises Viagra on TV.

MOST DANGEROUS OPPONENT

ANDREAS MOLLER. Despite earning more vitriol than any German player ever in the history of clashes between the two nations, his masterful midfield play was a lesson to all in how to dominate the middle third. He also had the bottle to convert that crucial penalty.

blasted home for 3-0 with half an hour left. Inside two minutes it was 4-0 and England was blissed out (man). Van der Sar saved from Anderton but couldn't hold the ball, which Sheringham lashed into the net. Kluivert came on as a substitute and although his goal was a consolation for the Dutch, it was no consolation for Scotland who were pipped to qualification by goals scored by the men in orange (they and the Dutch ended the group stage level on goal difference).

LET'S BLITZ FRITZ (DAILY MIRROR)

The English media hailed their team's inevitable progress to the final after the demolition of the Dutch. But a poor quarter-final, in which Spain incorrectly had a Salinas goal ruled out, and another 30 minutes of scrappy extra-time football meant a penalty shoot-out. Amazingly, England won it when David Seaman denied Miguel Nadal to set up a semi-final with Germany.

You could have bet that it would go to penalties. Alan Shearer put England ahead inside three minutes but Kuntz equalised 13 minutes later. Another 77 minutes failed to separate the sides and it went to extra-time.

In truth, both teams could have won it; Anderton hit the post, Seaman brilliantly denied Moller, Gazza was inches from scoring and Kuntz had a 'goal' disallowed.

Ten men stepped up to the plate, 10 men scored. And then Gareth Southgate put his penalty too close to the German keeper, Kopke. Andreas Moller converted the deciding kick before taking an inappropriate and thoroughly arrogant strut across the pitch. One could

England 'coach' receives a trophy shock! Fair Play Award at Euro '96

EUROPEAN CHAMPIONSHIPS 1996

GROUP A WINNERS: ENGLAND

England P3/W2/D1/L0/F7/A2
England 1 [Shearer] v Switzerland 1 [Turkilmaz pen]
8 June 1996 (Wembley)
Scotland 0 v England 2 [Shearer, Gascoigne]
15 June 1996 (Wembley)
Holland 1 [Kluivert] v England 4 [Shearer 2 (1 pen), Sheringham 2]
18 June 1996 (Wembley)

QUARTER-FINAL

England 0 v Spain 0 [AET]
England won 4-2 in a penalty shoot-out
22 June 1996 (Wembley)

SEMI-FINAL

England 1 [Shearer] v Germany 1 [Kuntz] [AET]
England lost 5-6 in penalty shoot-out, Southgate missed
26 June 1996 (Wembley)

THE FINAL

Germany 2 [Bierhoff 2] v Czech Republic 1 [Berger pen] [AET]
Germany won with a golden goal in the 5th min of extra-time
30 June 1996 (Wembley)

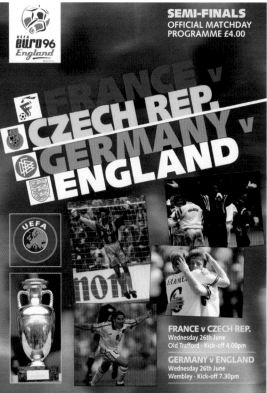

not imagine Gazza doing the same in different circumstances. Oh no.

When it was over, the general consensus was that the football in Euro '96 had been mediocre and that Germany, who won the trophy with a Golden Goal (the first time ever a major tournament had been settled in that way), was the best team of a bad bunch.

England did win the 'Fair Play' award, though.

ABOVE RIGHT: It was all going so well when these were printed

RIGHT: The single sleeve for Three Lions. All together now... or maybe not

NO CAP WONDERS

Despite the best efforts of Sven Goran Eriksson to cap every single eligible English football player during his reign as England manager, there are a couple of players who, surprisingly, didn't make it into an England shirt. Here are some personal selections of those players who should have played for England, but didn't.

JASON DODD

Southampton ('89–'05), Plymouth Argyle ('04 loan), Brighton & Hove Albion ('05–'06)

Played 454 games for Southampton. That unusual thing in modern-day football being a one-club man (but for his final year), Dodd holds the record for most appearances for one team in the Premiership (329) without being capped.

JIMMY GREENHOFF

Leeds Utd ('63–'68), Birmingham City ('68–'69), Stoke City ('69–'76), Man Utd ('76–'80), Crewe Alexandria ('80–'81) Toronto Blizzard ('81), Port Vale ('81–'83), Rochdale ('83–'84)

Scored 33 goals in 136 appearances for Leeds, 76 in 274 for Stoke, 36 in 123 for Man Utd. Won the League Cup with Stoke in 1972 and the FA Cup with Man Utd in 1977.

SUBS

GK Nicky Weaver: Mansfield Town ('94–'97) Man City ('97–)

Julian Dicks: Birmingham ('85–'88), West Ham ('88–'93, '94–'99) Liverpool ('93–'94). Everything Danny Mills wanted to be.

Kevin Nolan: Bolton Wanderers ('97–)

Kevin Davies: Chesterfield ('93–'97), Southampton ('97–'98, '00–'03), Blackburn Rovers ('98–'00), Bolton Wanderers ('03–)

STEVE BRUCE

Gillingham ('77–'84), Norwich City ('84–'87), Man Utd ('87–'96), Birmingham City ('96–'98), Sheff Utd ('98–'99)

Scored 51 goals in 414 games for Man Utd where he won three Premierships, two FA and a League Cup (also won with Norwich), plus the ECWC and UEFA Super Cup. Scored 19 in a season for Man Utd, most penalties. And one England 'B' cap.

BILLY BONDS

Charlton Athletic ('64–'67), West Ham Utd ('67–'88)

Scored 48 goals in 655 games for West Ham, where he became captain after Bobby Moore. Won the FA Cup in 1975 and 1980, led the Hammers to the European Cup Winners Cup final in 1976 and was the best midfield partner for Trevor Brooking at a time when England couldn't find one.

GARY SHAW

Aston Villa ('78–'88), FC Copenhagen ('88), Klagenfurt ('88–'90), Walsall ('90), Kilmarnock ('90), Shrewsbury ('90–'91)

Usually averaged a goal every three games. If not for injury he'd probably have averaged more. He won the 1982 European Cup, nine England Youth caps and seven at Under 21 level, was voted PFA Young Player of the Year in 1981.

GK: TONY COTON

Man City ('78–'84), Watford ('84–'90), Man City ('90–'96)
Sunderland ('96–'99)

Made 621 first-team appearances and even scored a goal
(for Man City). Cost a total of £2.4 million in transfer fees
and at the time of writing worked as a goalkeeping coach at
Man Utd, suggesting he knew the game. One England 'B' cap.

DEREK MOUNTFIELD

Tranmere Rovers ('80–'82), Everton ('82–'88), Aston Villa ('88–
'91), Wolves ('91–'94), Carlisle ('94–'95), Northampton ('95),
Walsall ('95–'98), Scarborough ('98)

Scored 38 goals in 445 career games. Won two First Division
titles and an FA Cup with Everton. Had a scoring record of one
every 5.6 games, which is almost better than Heskey.

DAVID BURROWS

WBA ('86–'88), Liverpool ('88–'93), West Ham ('93–'94), Everton
('94–'95), Coventry ('95–'00), Birmingham ('00–'02), Sheff Wed
('02–'03)

Scored 38 goals in 449 career games at left back. Won the
League Championship and FA Cup at Anfield and earned just
three 'B' caps for England.

HOWARD KENDALL

Preston North End ('63–'67), Everton ('67–'74), Birmingham City
('74–'77), Stoke City ('77–'79), Blackburn Rovers ('79–'81)

Scored 21 goals in 229 First Division games for Everton,
where he played alongside Alan Ball and Colin Harvey, and
won the First Division in 1970. At Birmingham he scored 16
in 115 games, feeding Trevor Francis passes to score from.

PETER BEAGRIE

Middlesbrough ('83–'85), Sheff Utd ('86–'88), Stoke ('88–'89),
Everton ('89–'94), Man City ('94–'97), Bradford ('97–'01)
Scunthorpe ('01–'06), Grimsby Town ('06)

A real left-footed winger who could beat defenders and cross
the ball, he was still at the top of his game when the Turnip
could have done with such a player.

MIKE NEWELL

Crewe ('82–'83, '99), Wigan ('83–'86), Luton ('86–'87), Leicester
('87–'89), Everton ('89–'91), Blackburn Rovers ('91–'96),
Birmingham ('96–'97), Aberdeen ('97–'99), Doncaster ('99–'00),
Blackpool ('00–'01)

Between 1992 and 1996 he was the best strike partner Alan
Shearer had and they won the Premiership title for Blackburn.

MANAGER: BRIAN CLOUGH (NOTTS FOREST)

Hartlepool ('65–'67), Derby County ('67–'73), Brighton &
Hove Albion ('73–'74), Leeds Utd ('74), Notts Forest ('75–'93)

He won the Second Division and First Division with Derby, the
First Division and two European Cups plus four League Cups
with Notts Forest and was always the people's choice when
England needed a new manager. Given how many silk purses
he made out of sow's ears at Forest and Derby one can only
wonder what he could have done with England in the '70s.

WORLD CUP FRANCE 1998

COME ON, EILEEN

When Glenn Hoddle took control of England from Terry Venables, the national team had ended the last two competitions they'd qualified for by going out on penalties. They'd also lost their last two managers through sustained vindictive tabloid campaigns. Surely things would be different this time around for a young, adventurous and seemingly well-liked manager?

There was great optimism going into France '98. It was based on the success of a new generation of young players centred around the Manchester United contingent who were dominating the Premiership (Gary Neville, Paul Scholes and David Beckham). There were also experienced campaigners like Alan Shearer and Teddy Sheringham plus the explosive pace of Michael

Owen to add to the expectations of English success.

Hoddle had expressed doubts about Owen's inclusion, saying he 'wasn't a natural striker'. But the teenager's 18 goals, making him joint leading scorer in the Premiership, and a press-led national clamour for his inclusion made it difficult to leave him at home.

England had qualified for the finals top of their group (2) along with Italy, having lost just one game at home to Italy and winning the rest except for a draw in Italy. They had scored 15 goals and conceded just two, so the news that they were in a first round group with Romania, Tunisia and Colombia, with two progressing to the Round of 16, was cause for optimism.

England began the tournament with a 2-0 win over Tunisia, but lost the next match 2-1 to Romania.

In a dramatic reconstruction of a South American religious painting, David Beckham plays Judas to Kim Nielsen's Peter. Simeone (R) is Paul

ENGLAND SQUAD

	CLUB	AGE	CAPS	GOALS
GOALKEEPERS				
David Seaman	Arsenal	34	40	
Nigel Martyn	Leeds	31	7	
Tim Flowers	Blackburn	31	11	
FULL BACKS				
Gary Neville	Man Utd	23	27	
Graham Le Saux	Chelsea	29	25	1
CENTRE BACKS				
Gareth Southgate	Aston Villa	27	25	
Tony Adams	Arsenal	31	51	4
Sol Campbell	Tottenham	23	16	
Martin Keown	Arsenal	31	18	1
Rio Ferdinand	West Ham	19	3	
MIDFIELDERS				
David Beckham	Man Utd	23	15	
Paul Ince	Liverpool	30	39	2
Rob Lee	Newcastle	32	17	2
David Batty	Newcastle	29	31	
Paul Scholes	Man Utd	23	7	3
Darren Anderton	Tottenham	26	18	5
Steve McManaman	Liverpool	26	21	
FORWARDS				
Alan Shearer	Newcastle	27	39	18
Teddy Sheringham	Man Utd	32	33	9
Michael Owen	Liverpool	18	5	1
Paul Merson	Middlesbro'	30	18	2
Les Ferdinand	Tottenham	31	17	5

Previous pages: BACK L-R: Unknown, Seaman, Sheringham, Beckham, Merson, Keown, Flowers, Martyn, Batty, Southgate Le Saux, Ferdinand R, Hoddle, Anderton, Shearer, Gorman, Ferdinand L, Clemence, Unknown, McManaman. FRONT L-R: Lee, Campbell, Adams, Owen, Neville G, Scholes, Taylor

THE MANAGER: GLENN HODDLE

Glenn Hoddle became the youngest ever England manager at 38 when he was appointed by the FA in May 1996. Terry Venables was still in charge and about to lead the team out for their games in the 1996 European Championships at the time. Hoddle's appointment didn't come into effect until after the Euros, but you have to wonder who in the England camp knew about his appointment. Did Venables or the team?

Hoddle won 53 caps, scoring eight goals. But he wasn't a 'typical' English footballer. Tracking back was not something that he thought a man of his passing ability should have to do, it seemed.

He began his managerial career with Swindon, as player-manager in 1991. He got them into the Premiership before taking over as Chelsea player-manager in 1993, retiring as a player in 1995. On becoming England manager he immediately put David Beckham into the starting line-up for the opening World Cup '98 qualifier in Moldova, but introduced a 3-5-2 formation which drew a comment of being 'overly defensive' from Venables.

After losing a qualifier at home to Italy, the FA gave him a vote of confidence, even if England failed to qualify for France '98. Everyone else knew he'd never last, of course.

Hoddle's biggest mistake was not dropping Paul Gascoigne, but appointing a faith healer, Eileen Drury, to the England coaching staff. Hoddle, a born-again Christian, met Eileen when he had a hamstring injury in his playing days. Although he wouldn't let her touch his leg when she was introduced to him at Spurs, he claimed that she had carried out 'absent healing', and the next day his leg was fine.

Eileen became the first faith healer to be put on the FA payroll (as far as we know). Sadly, she couldn't heal the team's recurring illness of penalty misses.

HODDLE'S ENGLAND RECORD 1 SEPT 1996 – 30 JUNE 1998

P	W	D	L	F	A	WIN %
24	15	4	5	36	11	62.5

WHY WAS HE THERE?

DARREN ANDERTON. His nickname was 'Sicknote' and he'd played just 15 times for his club (Spurs) in the domestic season leading up to the finals, and eight of those was as a substitute. He did score the opening goal against Colombia, but he didn't complete the game (nor the one against Argentina). But then he only managed 19 full games for England in his seven years of being picked, scoring just three times in competitive matches.

WHY WASN'T HE THERE?

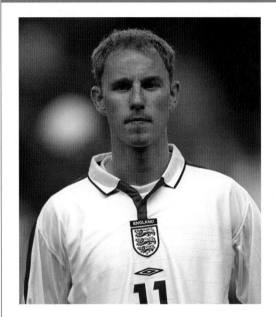

NICKY BUTT was far more consistent than David Batty and less headstrong and so less likely to be booked or sent off. Alternatively, Des Walker could have provided better cover at full back, centre half and midfield. Chris Sutton scored a total of 21 goals, 19 in the Premiership that season, and would not only have offered an in-form alternative to Les Ferdinand up-front but would also have provided better cover at centre half than 32-year-old Martin Keown.

A 2-0 win over Colombia and second place in Group G meant a Second Round game against Argentina. According to legend, Hoddle simply muttered the words 'Hand of God' to his team before they went out to meet the Argentines. It must have scared the hell out of them because they were 1-0 down inside five minutes when Batistuta converted a penalty after Simeone fell over Seaman. Four minutes later Shearer's penalty, awarded after Owen was fouled, equalised. Owen showed almost supersonic acceleration five minutes later to score a blistering goal and put England ahead. Scholes missed a chance for 3-1 and Argentina equalised in time added on to the first half. Two minutes into the second half David Beckham was felled by Simeone (not for the first time in the game) and as he lay prone, the Englishman flicked out a petulant foot at the Argentine, who went down as if shot. Beckham was dismissed for violent behaviour. My, how we all laughed.

MOST DANGEROUS ENGLAND PLAYER

MICHAEL OWEN. Without question. The opening game against Tunisia was only his sixth cap and few international managers had seen him in action. Owen burst onto the world scene in a blur of speed and scored twice in France. His scoring record since France '98 (33 goals in 71 games) bears out his importance to England.

MOST DANGEROUS OPPONENT

SIMEONE. Not only did the Argentine thespian fall as if hit by a sniper after Beckham's flick at him in the Round of 16 game, earning Beckham his red card, but he had earlier also fallen over Seaman to earn the penalty by which Argentina opened the scoring.

MOST OVERRATED ENGLAND PLAYER

STEVE McMANAMAN. Again (see Euro '96). Never really fulfilled his potential as an England player, drifted in and out of games too often for most fans and had a very annoying haircut. Maybe if he'd kept it out of his eyes he wouldn't have meandered down so many blind alleys on the pitch, before hitting the ball into the crowd.

Ten-man England went on to almost win the game but a Campbell headed goal was ruled out for a Shearer foul on the 'keeper. Extra-time came and went with no more goals and so for the third time running England faced a penalty shoot-out.

That England had not practised spot kicks was annoying enough, but to learn later that David Batty, who missed the decisive penalty, after Paul Ince's miss, had never in his professional career taken a penalty, caused millions of people back home to wonder what Glenn Hoddle was thinking. It was not to be the last time the nation wondered what he was thinking...

WORLD CUP 1998 QUALIFYING

GROUP 2 WINNERS: ENGLAND

England P8/W6/D1/L1/F15/A2
Moldova 0 v England3 [Barmby, Gascoigne, Shearer]
1 Sept 1996 (Moldova)
England 2 [Shearer 2] v Poland 1 [Citko]
9 Oct 1996 (Wembley)
Georgia 0 v England 2 [Sheringham, Ferdinand]
9 Nov 1996 (Georgia)
England 0 v Italy 1 [Zola]
12 Feb 1997 (Wembley)
England 2 [Sheringham, Shearer] v Georgia 0
30 April 1997 (Moldova)
Poland 0 v England 2 [Shearer, Sheringham]
31 May 1997 (Poland)
England 4 [Scholes, Wright 2, Gascoigne] v Moldova 0
10 Sept 1997 (Wembley)
Italy 0 v England 0
11 Oct 1976 (Italy)

WORLD CUP 1998 FINALS

GROUP G WINNERS: ROMANIA

England 2nd P3/W2/D0/L1/F5/A2
England 2 [Shearer, Scholes] v Tunisia 0
15 June 1998 (Marseille)
Romania 2 [Moldovan, Petrescu] v England 1 [Owen]
22 June 1998 (Toulouse)
Colombia 0 v England 2 [Anderton, Beckham]
26 June 1998 (Lens)

ROUND OF 16

Argentina 2 [Batistuta, Zanetti] v England 2 [Shearer (pen), Owen] [AET] Argentina won 4-3 penalty shoot-out, Ince and Batty missed
30 June 1998 (Saint-Etienne)

THE FINAL

Brazil 0 v France 3 [Zidane (2), Petit]
12 July 1998 (Saint-Denis, Paris)

EUROPEAN CHAMPIONSHIPS
BELGIUM/NETHERLANDS 2000

DOUBLE DUTCH

It was the first major international tournament held jointly by Belgium and Holland and proved to be one of the most memorable European competitions, with entertaining football producing a record 85 goals from 51 matches. England contributed to the entertainment. With Kevin Keegan having rescued qualification from the hands of mystic Glenda Hoddle, the national team became exciting to watch and wholly unpredictable. Keegan managed like he played, on the attack and with lots of emotion. Which is why he took only one recognised full back (Neville G), five central defenders, nine midfielders and six strikers – although only one was in double figures for England – to the Lowlands. Admittedly they had only sneaked into the finals via a play-off, but it was against Scotland and England had won 2-0 at Hampden, which is always fun. The return at Wembley wasn't as enjoyable, with the Scots winning through a goal by Anglo-Scot Don Hutchison, but it was enough to put England through and Scotland out.

England's opening match was a five-goal thriller, which ended 3-2 to Portugal. Fantastically, England led 2-0 with just 18 minutes gone and went on to lose – something that hadn't happened since Mexico '70.

Neville P makes the kind of tackle that any dedicated left back would make in the box. He wasn't actually a left back, but no-one else would play there

ENGLAND SQUAD

	CLUB	AGE	CAPS	GOALS
GOALKEEPERS				
David Seaman	Arsenal	36	57	
Nigel Martyn	Leeds	33	13	
Richard Wright	Arsenal	22	1	
FULL BACKS				
Gary Neville	Man Utd	25	36	
Phil Neville	Man Utd	23	26	
CENTRE BACKS				
Tony Adams	Arsenal	33	63	5
Gareth Barry	Aston Villa	19	2	
Sol Campbell	Tottenham	25	33	
Martin Keown	Arsenal	33	30	1
Gareth Southgate	Aston Villa	29	36	1
MIDFIELDERS				
David Beckham	Man Utd	25	31	1
Paul Ince	Middlesbro'	32	50	2
Steve McManaman	Real Madrid	28	28	2
Paul Scholes	Man Utd	25	24	9
Dennis Wise	Chelsea	33	16	1
Steven Gerrard	Liverpool	20	1	
FORWARDS				
Nick Barmby	Everton	26	13	3
Emile Heskey	Leicester	22	7	1
Michael Owen	Liverpool	20	19	6
Kevin Phillips	Sunderland	26	5	
Alan Shearer	Newcastle	29	60	28
Robbie Fowler	Liverpool	25	14	3

Previous page: BACK L-R: Keown, Southgate, Campbell, Barry, Taylor, Wright, Heskey, McManaman, Ince, Martyn, Adams, Gerrard, Beckham, Seaman, Neville G, Neville P, Phillips. FRONT L-R: Owen, Wise, Keegan, Shearer, Fowler, Barmby, Scholes

THE MANAGER: GLENN HODDLE (TO FEB 1999)

After the 1998 World Cup Hoddle published his diary of the tournament. David Seaman said that because the players were aware he was writing it, none of them would approach the manager with any problems in case they ended up in print. While publicising the book Hoddle suggested that disabled people might be suffering a punishment for sins that they'd committed on a previous life.

An unnamed senior England player remarked of him that 'If he was chocolate he would eat himself'. The Prime Minister said that he thought that Hoddle should go. And in February 1999 he did.

HODDLE'S ENGLAND RECORD 5 SEPT 1998 – 18 NOV 1998

P	W	D	L	F	A	WIN %
4	2	1	1	6	1	50

KEVIN KEEGAN (FEB 1999–OCT 2000)

Originally Keegan had said he'd take charge for four matches but then decided to take the job full time and so left his day job managing Fulham. As any Fulham or Newcastle fan would tell you (and you couldn't stop them once they got started), you'd never be sure if a team managed by Keegan would win, but you knew that they'd score. Under Keegan's control England failed to score in just three of their 18 games – although three of them came in the qualifiers for Euro 2000 – and he finished with a goal difference of +11 from as many draws as wins (seven). When the team lost you didn't seem to mind as much as when they'd lost under Hoddle or Taylor because at least they'd been entertaining.

KEEGAN'S ENGLAND RECORD 27 MARCH 1999 – 7 OCT 2000

P	W	D	L	F	A	WIN %
18	7	7	4	26	15	38.8

DENNIS WISE. A goalscoring midfielder, which Wise always was at club level, is greatly desirable at international level. But after scoring a debut goal, against Turkey, he didn't register another in his next 20 England appearances. And since he didn't score any goals, could get himself in an argument in an empty room and had that mad stare, why was he there? Because he was the only player who physically looked up to boss Kevin Keegan, possibly?

ANDY COLE was injured, according to Kevin Keegan, which is why he rarely selected him. Despite playing in the 0-0 with Sweden in the qualifiers and in the 2-0 win over Scotland, Cole didn't play under Keegan again until his last two matches. Yet Andy managed to score 19 goals as Man Utd retained their Premiership title, for a third time in succession in 2000. He also helped Utd to win a historic treble of Premiership, FA Cup and Champions League trophy in 1999.

With Germany held 1-1 by Romania the game between them and England became crucial for both countries. The only goal of the game, by Shearer, gave England their first competitive win over the Germans since the World Cup triumph in 1966 (the 1985 victory in the Azteca 2000 tournament doesn't count). Of course it provoked a marvellous dawning of false hope among press and fans alike, that England might go on to win the competition.

The team went into the final game of Group A needing just a draw against Romania to reach the quarter-finals. But things started badly in the warm-up when number one keeper David Seaman injured his ponytail and so Nigel Martyn started. Things got worse when the tournament's youngest player, 19-year-old Cristian Chivu, put Romania ahead, but England hit back to lead at the interval. While Keegan would have loved it, just loved it, if his team could have held on to

MOST DANGEROUS ENGLAND PLAYER

ALAN SHEARER. He scored eight goals in England's 11 games of the Euro 2000 campaign, and most importantly, he hit the winner against Germany which put them at the bottom of the group instead of England. **PAUL SCHOLES** runs him close, though, having scored six in the 11 games and all from midfield, including a hat-trick against Poland and both at Hampden Park to win qualification.

MOST DANGEROUS OPPONENT

LOUIS FIGO, in midfield for Portugal, was everything Beckham, McManaman, and Ince were not. Poised, elegant, incisive and inventive, he scored goals as well as made them for other players. Strong and supremely well balanced, he could ride tackles, go past players without being especially quick and pinpoint crosses.

MOST OVERRATED ENGLAND PLAYER

NICK BARMBY scored nine goals in 37 Premiership games in the season building up to Euro 2000. So perhaps it was his three goals in 13 internationals that bought him his ticket to Belgium/Holland? Or was it, as with Wise, that because he was small, Keegan saw something in him that reminded him of a short, nippy striker from the 1970s?

the win, or even a draw, they couldn't do either. Phil Neville – at left back though usually a midfielder for his club – made a reckless lunge at Moldovan and gave away a penalty which Ganea put away to win the match.

The nation burned their flags of St George in town squares across the land and the media called Keegan naive. After he'd sulked for four months, Keegan quit following England's loss in their last game at Wembley Stadium 0-1 to Germany (a World Cup qualifier). He said that he wasn't big enough for the job.

EUROPEAN CHAMPIONSHIPS 2000 QUALIFYING

GROUP 5 WINNERS: SWEDEN

England 2nd P8/W3/D4/L1/F14/A4 (qualified via play-off)

Sweden 2 [Andersson, Mjalby] v England 1 [Shearer]

5 Sept 1998 (Stockholm)

England 0 v Bulgaria 0

10 Oct 1998 (Wembley)

Luxemburg 0 v England 3 [Owen, Shearer, Southgate]

14 Oct 1998 (Luxemburg City)

England 3 [Scholes (3)] v Poland 1 [Brzeczek]

27 March 1999 (Wembley)

England 0 v Sweden 0

5 June 1999 (Wembley)

Bulgaria 1 [Markov)] v England 1 [Shearer]

9 June 1999 (Sofia)

England 6 [Shearer (3), McManaman (2), Owen] v Luxemburg 0

4 Sept 1999 (Wembley)

Poland 0 v England 0

8 Sept 1999 (Warsaw)

Scotland 0 v England 2 [Scholes (2)]

13 Nov 1999 (Glasgow)

England 0 v Scotland 1 [Hutchinson]

17 Nov 1999 (Wembley)

EUROPEAN CHAMPIONSHIPS 2000 FINALS

GROUP A WINNERS: PORTUGAL (ROMANIA ALSO QUALIFIED)

England 3rd P3/W1/D0/L2/F5/A6 (eliminated)

Portugal 3 [Figo, Pinto, Gomes] v England 2 [Scholes, McManaman]

12 June 2000 (Eindhoven)

England 1 [Shearer] v Germany 0

17 June 2000 (Charleroi)

England 2 [Shearer pen, Owen] v Romania 3 [Chivu, Munteanu, Ganea pen)]

20 June 2000 (Charleroi)

THE FINAL

France 2 [Wiltord, Trezeguet] v Italy 1 [Delvecchio] [AET, 1-1 at 90 min]

2 July 2000 (Rotterdam)

ENGLAND DREAM TEAM

All things being equal, this is the best team that England could hope to field in a World Cup with the best chance of winning it. However, the competition would have to staged in England, all England games would have to be at Wembley and beer would have to be 2/- a pint (that's 20p in today's money).

PHIL NEAL ('76–'83, CAPS 50)

Northampton Town ('68–'74), Liverpool ('74–'85), Bolton Wanderers ('85–'89)

Right back, won 50 caps for England (5 goals). He won eight First Division titles, four European Cups, one UEFA Cup, and four consecutive League Cups, 1981–84, all with Liverpool. He was also Liverpool's penalty-taker.

STEVE COPPELL ('77–'83, CAPS 42)

Tranmere Rovers ('73–'75), Man Utd ('75–'83)

Signed for Tranmere so that he could finish a degree in economics at Liverpool University. Made 373 appearances for Man United (scoring 70 goals), 207 of them in consecutive games, which is still a club record for an outfield player. Won the 1977 FA Cup (against Liverpool), scored 7 for England.

SUBS

GK Peter Shilton ('70–'90, caps 125)
Wayne Rooney ('03–, caps 38 to March '07, goals 12)
Alan Shearer ('92–'00, caps 63, goals 30)
John Barnes ('83–'95, caps 79, goals 11)
Jimmy Greaves ('59–'67, caps 57, goals 44)

MANAGER: ALF RAMSEY ('63–'74)

Managed Ipswich Town ('55–'63), Birmingham City ('77–'78)
The most successful England manager of all time.
P113/W69/D27/L17/F224/A98/Win%: 61.1

BOBBY MOORE © ('62–'73, CAPS 108)

West Ham ('58–'74), Fulham ('74–'77), San Antonio Thunder ('77), Seattle Sounders ('78)

Hurst may have scored the goals but Moore lifted the trophy. Still holds the record for most outfield caps, and was captain for 90 of the games played. He didn't get a booking in any of them either. Died in 1993 of bowel cancer.

STEVEN GERRARD ('00–, CAPS 55 TO MAR '07)

Liverpool ('97–)

Won the FA Cup '01, '06, Champions League '06, the UEFA Cup '01, and League Cup '01, '03. PFA Young Player of the Year '01, PFA Player of the Year '06. First player to score in the League, UEFA, Champions League and FA Cup Finals. Only 12 goals for England, but this team doesn't include Lampard.

GARY LINEKER ('84–'92, CAPS 80)

Leicester City ('78–'84), Everton ('85–'86), Barcelona ('86–'89), Spurs ('89–'92), Grampus Eight ('92–'94)

Lineker scored 48 goals for England, including five hat-tricks. Got 95 in 194 league games for Leicester, 30 in 41 for Everton, 44 in 99 for Barcelona, 67 in 105 for Spurs. Won the '91 FA Cup, the '88 Spanish Cup and '89 ECWC at Barça.

GK: GORDON BANKS ('63–'72, CAPS 73)

Chesterfield ('55–'59), Leicester City ('59–'66), Stoke City ('66–'72), Cleveland Stokers (67), St Patrick's Athletic (77), Fort Lauderdale Strikers ('77–'78)

Made the save of the century against Pelé in 1970, and kept 35 clean sheets for England before a car accident left him with no sight in his right eye in 1972.

TONY ADAMS ('87–'00, CAPS 66)

Arsenal ('84–'00)

Captained Arsenal from the age of 21, made 504 league appearances, scored 32 goals, won two doubles ('98, '02), two other Premiership titles and another FA Cup. Scored five goals for, and captained, England 15 times. Played more games at Wembley for England than any other player (60).

STUART PEARCE ('87–'99, CAPS 78)

Wealdstone ('81–'83), Coventry ('83–'85), Notts Forest ('85–'97), Newcastle ('97–'99), West Ham ('99–'01), Man City ('01–'02)

A wholly left-footed full back. Was the 999th player picked for England, scored five goals, was captain 10 times, missed one of the semi-final penalties in 1990. Missed a penalty in his last game for Man City; has a career total of 99 goals.

BRYAN ROBSON ('80-'91, CAPS 90)

WBA ('75–'81) Man Utd ('81–'94), Middlesborough ('94–'96)

Joined Manchester United for a record £1.7 million, became longest-serving captain in the club's history. Won the Premier League '93, '94, the '91 ECWC and the FA Cup '83, '85 and '90. Only injuries prevented him from adding to his caps (64 as captain) and 26 goals scored for England.

BOBBY CHARLTON ('58–'70, CAPS 106)

Man Utd ('54–'73), Preston North End ('73–'75)

Arguably the most famous English footballer in the world, still the England scoring record holder (49). A Busby Babe, he won the First Division '57, '65 and '67, captained Utd to a European Cup win in '68, won the FA Cup '63 and holds club record of 757 games (249 goals). Also won a World Cup.

GEOFF HURST ('66–'72, CAPS 49)

West Ham ('59–'72), Stoke ('72–'75), WBA ('75–'76), Seattle Sounders ('76)

Still the only player to have scored a World Cup Final hat-trick. Won three different trophies in three consecutive years at Wembley ('64 FA Cup, '65 ECWC, '66 World Cup). Scored 252 in 499 games for West Ham, 24 for England.

England's Dream Team and World Cup-winning captain Bobby Moore demonstrates his unflappable style on the ball

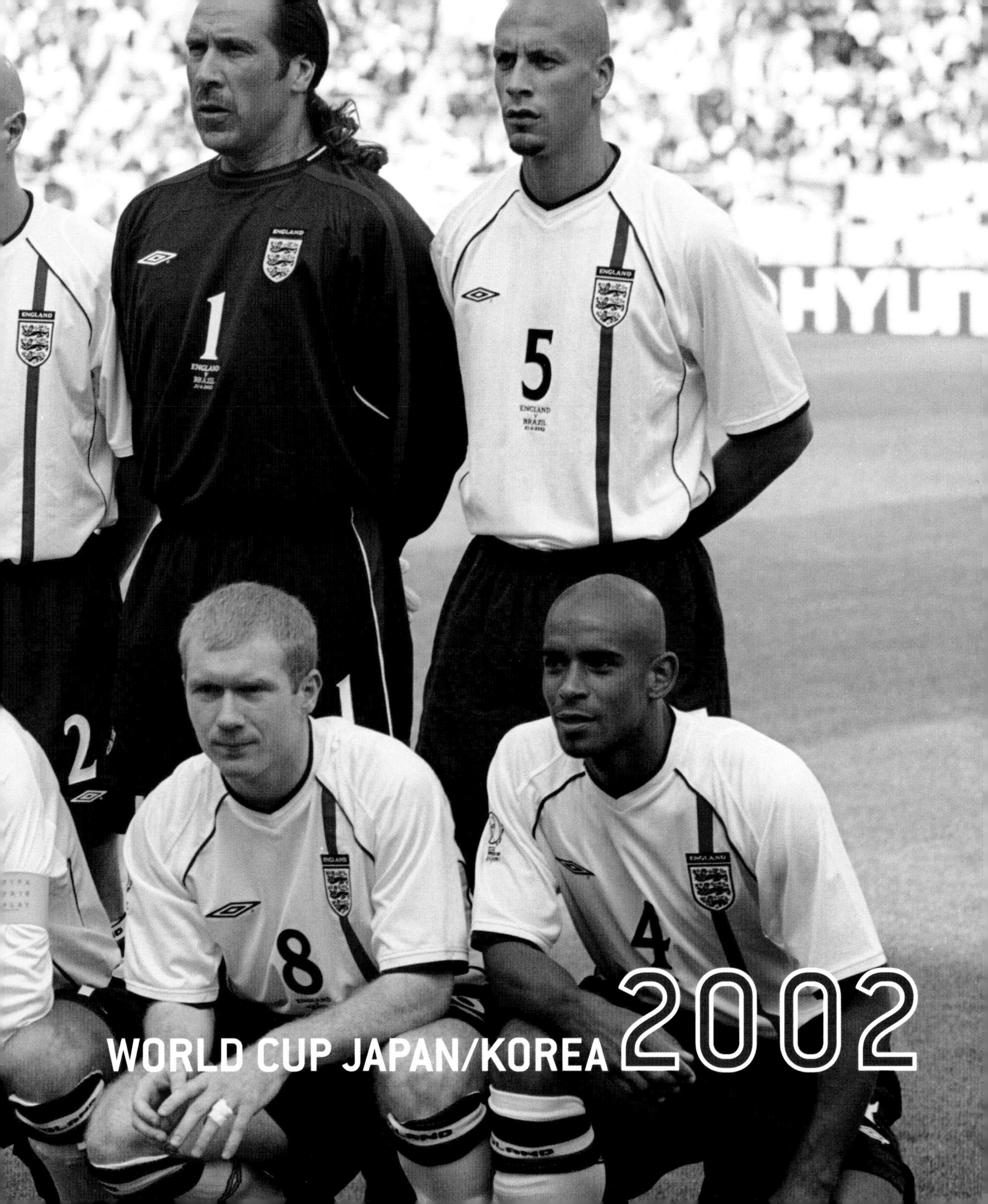

WORLD CUP JAPAN/KOREA 2002

'I WILL MAKE IT' (THE *DAILY EXPRESS*)

In 1970 we wuz robbed by a stolen bracelet and food poisoning. In 2002 we wuz robbed by a metatarsus – an English one at that.

The 2002 World Cup would be the eighth since Hurst's glorious hat-trick. After beating the Germans 5-1 in Munich during qualifying, the English media, with its usual restraint and level-headed analysis of England's chances of winning the trophy again, declared that, naturally, England would win it. Just as long as a certain metatarsal bone healed in time. That it belonged to Goldenballs, David Beckham (fractured during a Champions League game in which he played for Man Utd against Deportivo La Coruna), meant that it was front-page news everywhere. Even in medical journals. It wasn't only his either. His Old Trafford teammate (and best man at the Wedding of the Century © tabloids everywhere) Gary Neville also busted a pesky small bone in his foot before the competition, and he definitely wouldn't make it. No-one seemed to care too much about Gary's availability, except the rugged and uncompromising Danny Mills, a shaven-headed Englishman who would have had 'Made in England' tatooed on his forehead if he thought that it would get him a game for England at right back. As it turned out he didn't need to, since for some reason Sven the Manager decided that Mills would replace Neville.

Ever the PR man, Sven knew that he had no replacement for his captain and People's Favourite. Four years later Sven would include two players in a World Cup squad because he thought the tabloids would crucify him if he didn't. He set the precedent for that here. Beckham would never say no to a game and despite not being fully fit, travelled to the Land of the Rising Yen-for-Replica-Shirts.

Sadly for Liverpudlians, Steven Gerrard injured his groin in Liverpool's final Premiership game of the 2001/2002 season, and since the press were busy

The full England squad pose on the steps of their transport to Japan and Korea. Danny Murphy (4th from bottom) broke a metatarsal in training and returned home.

ENGLAND SQUAD

	CLUB	AGE	CAPS	GOALS
GOALKEEPERS				
David Seaman	Arsenal	38	68	
David James	West Ham	32	9	
Nigel Martyn	Leeds	35	23	
FULL BACKS				
Danny Mills	Leeds	25	7	
Ashley Cole	Arsenal	21	8	
Wayne Bridge	S'hampton	21	5	
CENTRE BACKS				
Rio Ferdinand	Leeds	23	22	
Gareth Southgate	Middlesbro'	31	49	1
Sol Campbell	Arsenal	27	46	
Wes Brown	Man Utd	23	6	
Martin Keown	Arsenal	35	43	
MIDFIELDERS				
David Beckham	Man Utd	27	49	6
Paul Scholes	Man Utd	27	44	13
Kieron Dyer	Newcastle	23	9	
Nicky Butt	Man Utd	27	18	
Owen Hargreaves	B Munich	21	6	
Joe Cole	West Ham	21	6	
Trevor Sinclair	West Ham	29	5	
FORWARDS				
Michael Owen	Liverpool	22	36	16
Emile Heskey	Liverpool	24	24	3
Teddy Sheringham	Tottenham	36	47	11
Robbie Fowler	Leeds	27	25	7

Previous page: BACK L-R: Owen, Campbell, Heskey, Mills, Seaman, Ferdinand. FRONT L-R: Butt, Cole, Beckham, Scholes, Sinclair line up before the game against Denmark, which they won 3-0.

THE MANAGER: SVEN GORAN ERIKSSON

When Sven Goran Eriksson was announced as the first foreign England manager, Jack Charlton said it was 'a terrible mistake', while PFA chief executive Gordon Taylor commented, 'It is a very sad day for English football and a terrible indictment of our national association.' However, as one wag in the national press put it, we'd had a turnip as a manager, so why not try a Swede as well?

Sven had been a right back in the Swedish Second Division until forced to retire through injury. He started his coaching career with Swedish Third Division club Degerfors before graduating to Gothenburg, where he won the 1981 League Championship and the 1982 UEFA Cup. Over the next 18 years he won the League Championships of Portugal and Italy, along with another 11 club trophies.

He set about ensuring qualification for the 2002 World Cup, with success. However, the press noted that he didn't know whether 4-4-2 or a 'diamond' formation suited England best. Nor did he pick players who could adapt to a change of tactics within a game. He also chose to play in-form players out of position.

Yet he did make the quarter-finals of the 2002 World Cup after only seven months in charge. However, it was reported that an England player who had been in the squad in Japan and Korea said of Sven's half-time talks that, 'when things were going wrong the players needed Winston Churchill – but we got Iain Duncan Smith.'

SVEN'S ENGLAND RECORD 28 FEB 2001 – 21 JUNE 2002

P	W	D	L	F	A	WIN %
20	10	7	3	33	14	50

WHY WAS HE THERE?

DANNY MILLS was the main beneficiary of Gary Neville's absence in Japan and Korea, since for some strange reason he was chosen as the Mancunian's replacement at full back. He was uncompromising in the way that so endears a player to the thug element among fans, but Mills was an average, no-frills English defender who couldn't cross a road, let alone provide a service for strikers.

WHY WASN'T HE THERE?

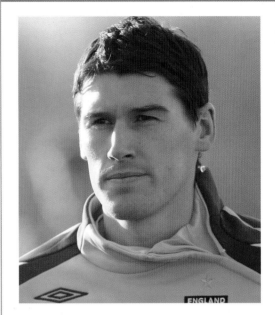

GARETH BARRY had already been capped six times at full international level. He was and remains among the best in the position of left wing-back. He could tackle like a left back, create like a midfielder and cross like a left winger. Throw in his versatility at centre back and the fact that he was likely to pop up with a goal, and you have five good reasons to question why Sven didn't take him East.

looking left, Sven felt comfortable enough to not include a crocked Gerrard in his squad.

Sports writers in England concerned themselves with filling England's left side of midfield. The absence of a natural wing-back polarised opinion between those who would select a player who was left footed and those who'd choose a right-footed player who could come inside and shoot or pass (such as Joe Cole) but would not produce crosses from that flank. Cole played on the left in the last friendly game before the finals, against

Cameroon, and so was apparently Sven's choice for the position at the World Cup.

'THE GROUP OF DEATH' (THE *SUN*)

When the tournament began England's first game in the 'Group of Death' was against Sweden. The metatarsal bone lasted an hour before being replaced by Kieron Dyer. Sven might as well have replaced Beckham with a training cone. With England leading courtesy of goalscoring machine Sol Campbell (first goal in 46

MOST OVERRATED ENGLAND PLAYER

EMILE HESKEY. Never punched his significant weight, at either club or international level. Perhaps he felt inhibited about using his ample physique in his role as a striker for fear of being punished by referees. He could have been an England regular for years – and it seemed as if he would, much to everyone but his own despair – but when it was finally pointed out that he had 'striker' in his job description and that they were expected to score goals, he was finally dropped. After winning the last of his 43 caps against France in 2004 his goal tally for England stood at five.

games), Danny Mills took it upon himself to give the Swedes a chance. His chest pass failed to reach goalkeeper Seaman and Alexandersson nipped in to level the scores. England then began to give the ball away regularly and lose their shape, but still managed a draw. In the second game of the group phase, England fought Argentina and miraculously won thanks to a penalty scored by the recovering metatarsal bone.

England won qualification with a dull goalless draw against Nigeria and set up a Second Round meeting with Denmark. Which was a stroke of luck, since the Danes decided that England needed to score a few goals in order to wind up English fans into a fever of optimism. Denmark let Owen, Ferdinand and even Emile Heskey score to earn a quarter-final against Brazil. Win this one, went English thinking, and we've won the Cup. Which goes to show how tenuous the grasp on reality was for English sports writers, fans and even players. They'd forgotten that you only won after contesting the actual final, but who could remember what that was like?

After the quarter-final, England blamed the heat (no food poisoning, though) for their inability to beat Brazil, who played the last half hour with 10 men. Michael Owen put England ahead midway through the first half, but 10 minutes of madness either side of the

MOST DANGEROUS OPPONENT

RONALDINHO masterminded Brazil's victory over England and was also behind his team's ultimate success in the final of the 2002 World Cup. Despite his dubious hairstyle and ever-present grin, it was obvious that here was a truly gifted, unique footballing talent. Not only did the ball stick to him, but it seemed to be mesmerised by his step-overs, feints and balletic moves. He looked thin but was substantial enough to ride tackles and even knock opponents off the ball. His like had never been seen in a World Cup. Pelé was stocky and physically different, as was Maradona. Only George Best could really have been compared with Ronaldinho. Big Phil Scolari, the Brazil manager and Bruce Forsyth fan (far left), turned down the chance to manage England after Sven had been pensioned off.

MOST DANGEROUS ENGLAND PLAYER

MICHAEL OWEN. Even though below par, he still managed to be the only England player to score more than one goal. Opposition teams identified him as the chief English goal threat and despite trying to mark him out of games, Owen's speed and agility ensured that he'd always get a couple of real chances in any match. That is, as long as his teammates could pass the ball to him and not the opposition, which sadly wasn't always the case.

interval did for Sven's men. David Beckham, on orders from his metatarsal bone, pulled out of a touchline challenge between a couple of Brazilians. The ball broke to Ronaldinho, who fed Rivaldo and he equalised. It was 1-1 at the break.

Five minutes into the second half Brazil were awarded a free-kick 45 yards from England's goal on the left touchline. Only Ronaldinho knows if he meant to float the free-kick over 'Safe Hands' in the England goal. He said afterwards that of course he intended to score. The ball caught Seaman too far off his line and

WORLD CUP 2002 QUALIFYING

GROUP 9 WINNERS: ENGLAND

England P8/W5/D2/L1/F16/A6 (Germany 2nd)

England 0 v Germany 1 [Hamann]

7 Oct 2000 (Wembley)

Finland 0 v England 0

11 Oct 2000 (Helsinki)

England 2 [Owen, Beckham] v Finland 1 [Riihilahti]

24 Mar 2001 (Liverpool)

Albania 1 [Rraklli] v England 3 [Owen, Scholes, Cole]

28 Mar 2001 (Tirane)

Greece 0 v England 2 [Scholes, Beckham]

6 June 2001 (Athens)

Germany 1 [Jancker] v England 5 [Owen 3, Gerrard, Heskey]

1 Sept 2001 (Munich)

England 2 [Owen, Fowler] v Albania 0

5 Sept 2001 (Newcastle)

England 2 [Sheringham, Beckham] v Greece 2 [Charisteas, Nikolaidis]

6 Oct 2001 (Manchester)

WORLD CUP 2002 FINALS

GROUP F WINNERS: SWEDEN

England 2nd: P3/W1/D2/L0/F2/A1

England 1 [Campbell] v Sweden 1 [Alexandersson]

2 June 2002 (Siatama)

Argentina 0 v England 1 [Beckham, pen]

7 June 2002 (Sapporo)

Nigeria 0 v England 0

12 June 2002 (Osaka)

THE ROUND OF 16

Denmark 0 v England 3 [Ferdinand, Owen, Heskey]

15 June 2002 (Niigata)

QUARTER-FINAL

England [Owen] 1 v Brazil 2 [Rivaldo, Ronaldinho]

21 June 2002 (Fukuroi)

THE FINAL

Brazil 2 [Ronaldo, 2] v 0 West Germany

30 June 2002 (Yokohama)

with that ridiculous ponytail flapping desperately behind him, he tried to back-peddle on realising that the ball was dropping over him, and under the bar.

Seven minutes later the sublime Ronaldinho was adjudged to have fouled Danny Mills (which was patently ridiculous) and was sent off for a second yellow card.

As if accepting the natural order of football, England then let Brazil stroll to their victory. Owen faded after his goal, Beckham's metatarsus twinged, Seaman proved closer to a career as a ballroom dancer than he'd let on and no-one could rescue England.

It's rumoured that the metatarsal bone auditioned for a couple of roles in Hollywood films after the World Cup, but they eventually went to Beckham's old foe Vinny Jones, instead. At least we beat the Germans 5-1 in Munich in qualifying. Did I mention that?

WHERE'S GEOFF?

By now Sir Geoff Hurst was promoting the paperback edition of his best-selling autobiography, *1966 And All That*. Sir Geoff had written a new chapter all about how he hoped Beckham and Owen would be collecting the World Cup at the end of the tournament. He was, he wrote, retiring from the limelight now. Sir Geoff still worked promoting various companies within the game, though, and was happy to be – if asked – part of any new English bid to host a future World Cup.

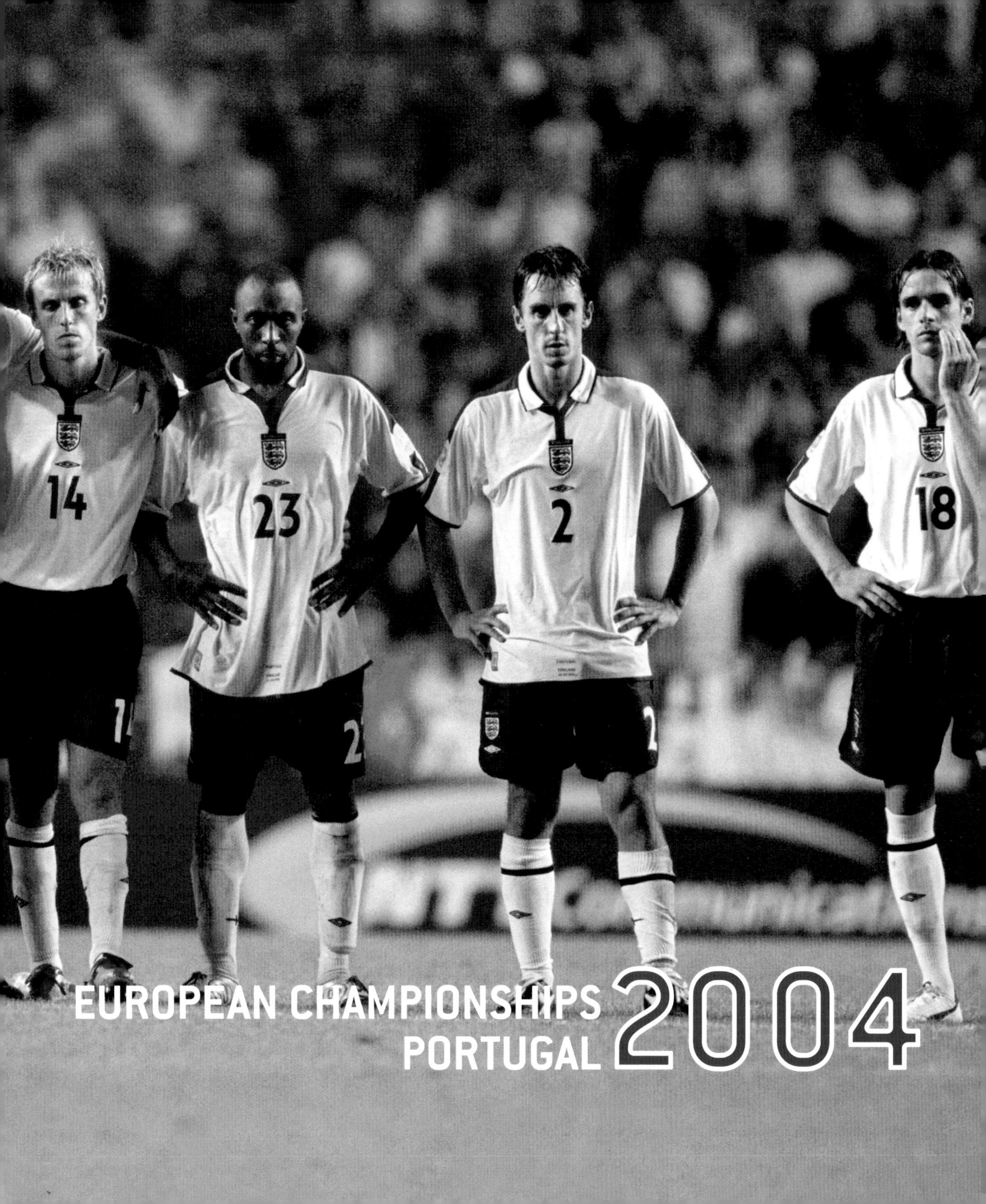

EUROPEAN CHAMPIONSHIPS PORTUGAL 2004

'ERIKSSON'S TINKERING CANNOT DISGUISE LACK OF WINNING' (THE *INDEPENDENT*)

England made it to Euro 2004 with Goldenballs wearing the captain's armband. Wayne Rooney's emergence as a raw but exciting goalscorer in the Premiership during 2002 was useful for Sven and England, too.

Other new faces in the England team appeared in their thousands during a seemingly endless round of friendlies that were played between qualifying games. Alan Smith, a striker who could also play in midfield, debuted and scored against Portugal in 2002. Jonathan Woodgate, Smith's Leeds teammate, and Canadian Owen Hargreaves (of Bayern Munich) also made their first appearances for the team.

Yet the first team almost picked itself at this time. In front of first-choice goalkeeper David James was a solid, if occasionally nervous, centre half pairing of John Terry and Rio Ferdinand, with Gary Neville and Ashley Cole either side. A four-man midfield of Steven Gerrard, David Beckham and Paul Scholes, plus AN Other, on the left was the supply line to the developing strike pair of Owen and Rooney. That left midfield slot proved to be something of a long-running problem, and although Joe Cole eventually won the struggle with Ledley King for the position, he was a right-footed player.

Another problem for England was the lack of goalscoring cover for Rooney and Owen. Jermaine Defoe missed out on the trip to Portugal in favour of Darius Vassell, who always performed better for the national team than he did for his club, Aston Villa. Sven was later to admit his error in omitting Defoe.

However, if the newspapers were to be believed (and who wouldn't?) Sven's build-up to Portugal was being compromised by the possibility of his joining Chelsea as manager. In order to focus their manager's mind on the job in hand, the Football Association decided that, instead of reminding Sven of his contractual obligations, they should extend his tenure

Sven and Mark Pallios meet some stewardesses on the way to Portugal

on improved terms. These were that he would be paid excessive amounts of money AFTER he left the job, which was to be after the 2006 World Cup.

'SVEN WILL WE EVER LEARN?' (*SUNDAY MIRROR*)

Euro 2004 kicked off with England losing to France, with Beckham missing a penalty. Wayne Rooney dominated the necessary win over Switzerland that came five days later, adding two goals to one by Gerrard. He repeated his brace against Croatia with Scholes and Lampard also scoring, but Croatia also scored two. In the quarter-final England faced the host nation and after 27

ENGLAND SQUAD

	CLUB	AGE	CAPS	GOALS
GOALKEEPERS				
David James	Man City	33	24	
Paul Robinson	Tottenham	24	5	
Ian Walker	Leicester	32	4	
FULL BACKS				
Phil Neville	Man Utd	27	48	
Gary Neville	Man Utd	29	63	
Ashley Cole	Arsenal	23	26	
Wayne Bridge	S'hampton	23	17	
CENTRE BACKS				
John Terry	Chelsea	23	8	
Sol Campbell	Arsenal	29	58	
Ledley King	Tottenham	23	5	
Jamie Carragher	Liverpool	26	12	
MIDFIELDERS				
Steven Gerrard	Liverpool	24	24	3
Frank Lampard	Chelsea	25	19	2
David Beckham	Real Madrid	29	68	12
Owen Hargreaves	B Munich	23	19	
Paul Scholes	Man Utd	29	62	13
Kieron Dyer	Newcastle	25	22	
Nicky Butt	Man Utd	29	35	
Joe Cole	Chelsea	22	17	2
FORWARDS				
Michael Owen	Liverpool	24	56	25
Wayne Rooney	Man Utd	18	13	5
Emile Heskey	Liverpool	26	42	5
Darius Vassell	Aston Villa	23	18	6

Previous page: L-R: Beckham, Owen, Lampard, Terry, Cole, Campbell, Neville P, Vassell, Neville G, and Hargreaves see their Golden Generation go out of a major tournament on penalties

THE MANAGER: SVEN GORAN ERIKSSON

Questions were asked about Sven's capability of leading England in the aftermath of yet another failure to progress beyond a quarter-final but attention quickly switched to the qualifying campaign for Euro 2004 and the fact that England swept through that campaign remains perhaps Eriksson's finest England achievement.

Unfortunately, the months before the Euro 2004 finals were dominated by off-the-field events surrounding the England Head Coach. A picture of him leaving the flat of Chelsea chief executive Peter Kenyon was splashed on the front page of the *Sun* along with accusations that Eriksson was being lined up to replace under-fire Claudio Ranieri as manager. When news of talks between Sven and other European clubs emerged in the aftermath of those revelations the FA responded by lengthening the Swede's contract and giving him a pay rise. But the public wasn't as forgiving of a man whose romantic dalliances with different women, alongside a long-term relationship with Nancy Dell'Olio, regularly made front page 'news'. The public wanted football headlines of the right sort from Sven, not cheap jokes about playing away.

Once again at a major tournament, however, in a quarter-final (against Portugal) England went out after failing in a penalty shoot-out. But Sven wasn't through yet, by golly, by gosh, oh no. There were still lots of women at the FA he hadn't met, after all.

SVEN'S ENGLAND RECORD 7 SEPT 2002 – 24 JUNE 2004

P	W	D	L	F	A	win %
22	12	6	4	43	24	55

(the draws total includes the 2-2 after 90 mins with Portugal)

WHY WAS HE THERE?

KIERON DYER has proved to be one of the most inconsistent players to play for England. Factor in a poor fitness record over the past decade and it's a wonder, with seven other midfield players, that he wasn't left behind and another striker taken. He is still (at time of writing) to score for England in 32 appearances.

WHY WASN'T HE THERE?

JERMAINE DEFOE would have been a better option than Emile William Ivanhoe Heskey, who went to Portugal having scored only five times for his country (his final total in 43 appearances). Whereas Defoe scored seven times in 14 games for Spurs in the Premiership season prior to Euro 2004 (as well as against Turkey in a qualifier).

minutes Rooney broke a bone in his foot. He limped off and – according to every newspaper and pub pundit in England – with him went England's Euro 2004 hopes. The 90 minutes ended with the teams at 1-1. After extra-time it was 2-2 and so the teams went into the inevitable penalty shoot-out.

Beckham fired his spot-kick over and Vassell had a weak shot saved by Ricardo. The Portuguese keeper then demonstrated how to score from 12 yards with probably the best penalty of the 11, to secure a 6-5 win for the hosts.

It was England's fourth penalty shoot-out elimination in a major competition since 1990.

England would just have to practice penalties for the next one, wouldn't they. Well, wouldn't they?

MOST DANGEROUS ENGLAND PLAYER

WAYNE ROONEY scored half of England's eight goals in the Group stage and two in the qualifiers. Although young and still raw, he wasn't known to the opposition, and so could – and did – surprise them with his running, power and shooting.

MOST DANGEROUS OPPONENT

RICARDO. Yes, he was a goalkeeper, but not only did the Portuguese stopper save the critical penalty from Vassell in the shoot-out, but he also scored the decisive spot-kick to dump England out of Euro 2004. Plus, he never lost a game against England and would again prove his worth as a penalty stopper in the 2006 World Cup.

MOST OVERRATED ENGLAND PLAYER

STEVEN GERRARD. Liverpool fans spoke of him as the next England captain after Beckham and raved about his ability to get from box to box, score goals, tackle and pass perfectly. Yet in Portugal his best pass went to Thierry Henry and his numerous attempts at spraying 30-yard balls invariably found their way either to the opposition or into touch. Maybe he was trying to impress Chelsea, who he was rumoured to be joining for the 2004–05 season, the little tease.

EUROPEAN CHAMPIONSHIPS 2004 QUALIFYING

GROUP 7 WINNERS: ENGLAND

England P8/W6/D2/L0/F14/A5

Slovakia 1 [Nemeth] v England 2 [Beckham, Owen]
12 Oct 2002 (Bratislava)

England 2 [Beckham, Gerrard] v Macedonia 2 [Sakiri, Trajanov]
16 Oct 2002 (Southampton)

Lichtenstein 0 v England 2 [Owen, Beckham]
29 March 2003 (Vaduz)

England 2 [Vassell, Beckham] v Turkey 0
2 April 2003 (Sunderland)

England 2 [Owen(2)] v Slovakia 1 [Janocko]
11 June 2003 (Middlesborough)

Macedonia 1 [Hristov] v England 2 [Rooney, Beckham]
6 Sept 2003 (Skopje)

England 2 [Owen, Rooney] v Lichtenstein 0
10 Sept 2003 (Manchester)

Turkey 0 v England 0
11 Oct 2003 (Istanbul)

EUROPEAN CHAMPIONSHIPS 2004 FINALS

GROUP B WINNERS: FRANCE

England 2nd P3/W2/D0/L1/F8/A4

England 1 [Lampard] v France 2 [Zidane (2)]
13 June 2004 (Lisbon)

England 3 [Rooney (2), Gerrard] v Switzerland 0
17 June 2004 (Coimbra)

England 4 [Scholes, Rooney (2), Lampard] v Croatia 2 [Kovac, Tudor]
21 June 2004 (Lisbon)

QUARTER-FINAL

Portugal 2 [Postiga, Costa] v England 2 [Owen, Lampard]
[AET] Portugal won 6-5 on penalties. Beckham, Vassell missed
24 June 2004 (Lisbon)

THE FINAL

Portugal 0 v Greece 1 [Charisteas]
4 July 2004 (Lisbon)

WORLD CUP GERMANY 2006

FORTY YEARS OF HURT

And so, four decades after the singular triumph of 1966 England set off to Germany with a squad who were supposed to be the Golden Generation of English players. They were certainly the highest paid in history, as any quality tabloid sports writer would tell you. Were they, though, the boys to end 40 years of hurt?

Of course they weren't. But they did have a nice bunch of WAGs, whose every cocktail drunk and shop visited was displayed prominently in the world's more discerning newspapers. At least they took the pressure off Wayne Rooney's busted metatarsus. Everything from prayer to a specialised oxygen tank was employed to ensure that Wayne went to Germany. Despite his not having played a game for weeks, Wazza would always be included if he could walk unaided, simply because he was the nation's Chosen One. The nation does not always choose the Right One, of course (in '66 it was Jimmy Greaves, in '82 it was Kevin Keegan, for instance), but when they choose the England manager does well to listen. So Wazza would be there and play, despite his club manager Alex Ferguson insisting that he wasn't ready.

However, besides the fact that Sven picked no fewer than eight midfielders, he chose just four strikers, who were Wazza, an equally unfit Michael Owen, a standard lamp named Peter Crouch, and a 17-year-old (Theo Walcott) who'd never played for his club's first team, let alone the international side.

In Lampard and Gerrard Sven had the two best goalscoring midfield players in the Premiership, maybe even Europe. Sadly, they had never complemented each other when playing together. Some people doubted (and still do, at time of writing) if they ever could. Paul Scholes had retired from international football, fed up with being forced to play as a winger for Sven in order to accommodate both Lampard and Gerrard, which left David Beckham as the squad's only fit goalscorer.

Sven and Brian Barwick do not meet stewardesses on the way to Germany

England had qualified for Germany top of their group, but it hadn't exactly been taxing. Still, once the tournament kicked off they cruised, unimpressively, into the quarter-finals. They beat Paraguay 1-0. The Standard Lamp and Gerrard scored in the last seven minutes to conquer the might of Trinidad and Tobago. But then disaster struck as England lost one of their four strikers in the draw with Sweden. Michael Owen's knee buckled under him, leaving Wazza, the Standard Lamp and The Boy to fire England to glory.

ENGLAND SQUAD

	CLUB	AGE	CAPS	GOALS
GOALKEEPERS				
Paul Robinson	Tottenham	26	21	
David James	Man City	35	34	
Scott Carson	Liverpool	20		
FULL BACKS				
Gary Neville	Man Utd	31	79	
Wayne Bridge	Chelsea	25	23	1
Ashley Cole	Arsenal	25	46	
CENTRE BACKS				
John Terry	Chelsea	25	24	
Rio Ferdinand	Man Utd	27	47	1
Sol Campbell	Arsenal	31	68	1
Jamie Carragher	Liverpool	28	25	
MIDFIELDERS				
Joe Cole	Chelsea	24	37	6
Frank Lampard	Chelsea	27	40	11
Stewart Downing	Middlesbro'	21	2	
Michael Carrick	Tottenham	24	6	
Jermaine Jenas	Tottenham	23	15	
Steven Gerrard	Liverpool	26	42	7
Owen Hargreaves	B Munich	25	30	
David Beckham	Real Madrid	31	89	17
Aaron Lennon	Tottenham	19	1	
FORWARDS				
Michael Owen	Newcastle	26	77	36
Wayne Rooney	Man Utd	20	29	11
Peter Crouch	Liverpool	25	7	5
Theo Walcott	Arsenal	17		

Previous page: L-R: Lampard, Ferdinand, Gerrard, Terry, Cole, Neville G, Hargreaves and Crouch see their Golden Generation go out of the World Cup on penalties. Again

THE MANAGER: SVEN GORAN ERIKSSON

Sven again took England to a major international tournament by annihilating the opposition in the qualifying games (except for Austria, of course. Oh, and Northern Ireland).

Sven then enigmatically bemused most of us with his curious player selection for the finals, especially by picking Theo Walcott, a 17-year-old who had only just left Championship side Southampton for Arsenal.

Sven went on to field a barely fit Wayne Rooney as a lone striker in the quarter-final against Portugal and watched helplessly as England went out on penalties, again.

And so, after five and a half years of expensive failure to deliver anything other than places in quarter-finals, and at great cost to the FA, Sven was removed from his job. Still, he did only lose five competitive games while England manager. Unfortunately, they were all crucial ones. His peculiarly public romances, lack of emotional expression in interviews and inability to motivate players in the dressing room made him almost the polar opposite of the only England manager to have so far won anything as boss. That the FA replaced him with an Englishman (who was not first choice) and who has similar failings – he even had to admit to an extramarital affair before taking the job – is a sad endictment of the organisation's inability to fathom where the English game is going wrong.

SVEN'S ENGLAND RECORD 18 AUG 2004 – 1 JULY 2006

P	W	D	L	F	A	WIN %
25	18	3	4	46	19	72%

SVEN'S ENGLAND RECORD IN FULL 2001–2006

P	W	D	L	F	A	WIN %
67	40	17	10	128	61	59.7%

WHY WAS HE THERE?

THEO WALCOTT. The last great mystery of the reign of Sven. Why take a 17-year-old who had just joined Arsenal in a multi-million pound deal to the World Cup as one of only four recognised strikers, with two of the others being crocked and the third more resembling Bambi on ice than a professional goalscorer? Theo might have shown pace, trickery and scored goals in the Championship (all five of them in 23 games), but the defenders of Portugal and Sweden usually played at a somewhat higher level than that.

'WE WERE NOT GOOD ENOUGH, ESPECIALLY THE PENALTIES.' (SVEN GORAN ERIKSSON)

England almost went out in the Round of 16 to Ecuador and it took a Beckham free-kick, making him the first Englishman to score in three World Cup finals, to set up a quarter-final against Portugal.

Wazza, fit enough to play, got himself sent off just past the hour. Either for stepping on the private parts of Carvalho or for pushing clubmate Ronaldo just after that. England had to play most of the second half with 10 men. Oh, and David Beckham limped off 10 minutes before Wazza was dismissed, but it was going to be OK because England had brought on the Standard Lamp and still hadn't played The Boy. The game ground towards an almost inevitable penalty shoot-out with the score at 0-0, and with a minute remaining in extra-time, Sven played

MOST DANGEROUS ENGLAND PLAYER

PETER CROUCH. If he fell on you it could take weeks to disentangle from those arms and legs. It was only a shame that he stopped doing that 'robotic' dance after scoring because opponents would have willingly let him score just so they could see how it was done, up close. For his goal against footballing geniuses Trinidad & Tobago all Crouchy had to do was let the ball hit him as he fell over and it was in the back of the net. That's truly dangerous finishing.

MOST DANGEROUS OPPONENT

CRISTIANO RONALDO showed, despite his flawed character, that he was ready to become a worthy successor to Ronaldinho as the best player in the world. Pace, goals, vision and trickery, at the right moment, demonstrated he had the complete package, in terms of ability. As if to underline the point, he took that form into the following Premier League campaign with Manchester United where, with the boos of thousands of Britons ringing in his ears every time he got the ball, he scored priceless goals and set up countless others.

MOST OVERRATED ENGLAND PLAYER

Paul Robinson, Gary Neville, Ashley Cole, Rio Ferdinand, John Terry, David Beckham, Frank Lampard, Wayne Rooney, Steven Gerrard, Joe Cole, Peter Crouch, Jamie Carragher and Stewart Downing.

WORLD CUP 2006 QUALIFYING

GROUP 6 WINNERS: ENGLAND

England P10/W8/D1/L1/F16/A5

Austria 2 [Kollmann, Ivanschitz] v England 2 [Lampard, Gerrard]

4 Sept 2004 (Vienna)

Poland 1 [Zurawski] v England 2 [Defoe, Glowacki (o.g.)]

8 Sept 2004 (Chorzow)

England 2 [Lampard, Beckham] v Wales 0

9 Oct 2004 (Manchester)

Azerbaijan 0 v England 1 [Owen]

13 Oct 2004 (Baku)

England 4 [Cole J, Owen, Lampard, Baird (o.g.)] v N. Ireland 0

26 March 2005 (Manchester)

England 2 [Gerrard, Beckham] v Azerbaijan 0

30 March 2005 (Newcastle)

Wales 0 v England 1 [Cole J]

3 Sept 2005 (Cardiff)

N. Ireland 1 [Healey] v England 0

7 Sept 2005 (Belfast)

England 1 [Lampard] v Austria 0

8 Oct 2005 (Manchester)

England 2 [Owen, Lampard] v Poland 1 [Frankowski]

12 Oct 2005 (Manchester)

WORLD CUP 2006 FINALS

GROUP B WINNERS: ENGLAND

England P3/W2/D1/L0/F5/A2

England 1 [Gamarra (o.g.)] v Paraguay 0

10 June 2006 (Frankfurt)

England 2 [Crouch, Gerrard] v Trinidad & Tobago 0

15 June 2006 (Nuremburg)

Sweden 2 [Allback, Larsson] v England 2 [Cole J, Gerrard]

20 June 2006 (Cologne)

ROUND OF 16

England 1 [Beckham] v Ecuador 0

25 June 2006 (Stuttgart)

QUARTER-FINAL

England 0 v Portugal 0 (AET) Portugal won 3-1 in penalty shoot-out, Carragher, Lampard, Gerrard missed

1 July 2006 (Gelsenkirchen)

THE FINAL

Italy 1 [Materazzi] v France 1 [Zidane (pen)] (AET)
Italy won 5-3 in penalty shoot-out

9 July 2006 (Berlin)

his last card and threw on that renowned penalty-taker Jamie Carragher in place of Aaron Lennon. That's Jamie Carragher who has never scored a penalty in his professional career. He, Lampard and Gerrard all had their efforts saved, making Ricardo the first keeper in World Cup history to save three in a shoot-out. He very nearly made it four by getting a hand to Hargreaves' attempt, but the shoot-out ended 3-1 to Portugal.

For the sixth time in seven shoot-outs England had lost and for the third consecutive tournament our national team went out at the quarter-final stage. Wittily, the German paper *Bild* printed a step-by-step guide to taking penalties, in English, for our benefit.

Who said they don't have a sense of humour? David Beckham, in tears as he sat on the bench after the quarter-final, announced his resignation as skipper the next day. So did Sven.

In the aftermath of another England failure the FA offered the vacant England manager's job to Big Phil Scolari, who said 'No'. The FA then denied that they'd offered the job to him anyway, and set about interviewing suitable candidates. Stuart Pearce and Sam Allardyce said they'd love the job, but neither had won anything as managers, so the FA chose Steve McLaren instead. Maybe he knows how to practise taking penalties successfully...

ACKNOWLEDGEMENTS

Thanks to Mark Baber at AFS, Mal Peachey, Essential Works, John Richardson, Chief Football Writer *Sunday Express,* Forest Robertson, Scottish Football Statistician, Ceri Stennett FAW Historian, Mike Trusson FA Coach Tutor and founder of www.grassrootscoaching.com, The *Sunday Express,* Tony Cottee.

BIBLIOGRAPHY

The Best of Enemies England v Germany
David Downing (Bloomsbury 2001)
The Breedon Book of Premiership Records
Brian Beard (Breedon Publishing 2004)
Breedon Club Histories A Complete Record of:
Manchester City
Liverpool
Everton
Spurs
Sheffield Wednesday
Aston Villa
Huddersfield Town (all Breedon Publishing)
The Daily Telegraph Chronicle of Football
Norman Barrett (Carlton for Index Books, 2001)
The Encyclopaedia of Association Football
Maurice Golesworthy (Robert Hale Limited, 1976)
England The Quest for the World Cup
Clive Leatherdale (Desert Island Football Book/Two Heads Publishing, 1994)
The Essential History of England
Andrew Mourant and Jack Rollin (Headline, 2002)
Golden Heroes: 50 Seasons of Footballer of the Year
Dennis Signy and Norman Giller (Chameleon Books, 1997)
The Guinness Record of the World Cup 1930–94
Jack Rollin (Guinness Publishing, 1994)
The Hamlyn A-Z of British Football Records
Phil Soar (Hamlyn, 1981)
Moore on Mexico World Cup 1970
Bobby Moore as told to Kevin Moseley (Stanley Paul, 1970)
The PFA Premier and Football League Players' Records 1946–1998
Barry J Hugman (Queen Anne Press, 1999)
Pictorial History of English Football
Robert Jeffery with Mark Gonnella (Paragon, 2001)
Rothmans Football Year Book
Glenda Rollin and Jack Rollin (Headline)

Sixties Revisited
Jimmy Greaves with Norman Giller (Queen Anne Press, 1992)
Sky Sports Football Year Book 2003
Glenda Rollin and Jack Rollin (Headline, 2003)
The Sunday Times Illustrated History of Football
Chris Nawrat and Steve Hutchings (Reed International Books, 1994)
The Sunday Times Illustrated History of Football, The Post War Years
Chris Nawrat and Steve Hutchings (Reed International Books, 1995)
Wembley The FA Cup Finals 1923–2000
Glen Isherwood (Britespot, 2001)
World Cup Soccer
Michael Lewis (Moyer Bell, 1994)

Websites
www.4thegame.com
www.arseweb.com
www.englandfanzine.com
www.englandfootballonline.com
www.englandstats.com
www.footballanorak.com
www.newspaperarchive.com
www.planetworldcup.com
www.rsssf.com
www.redcafe.net
www.soccerbase.com
www.soccerfile.com
soccernet.espn.go.com
www.squarefootball.net
www.thinkexist.com
www.wikipedia.org

PLUS
My personal collection of football magazines, for which I have written over many years, and my pile of yellowing newspaper cuttings from the *Sunday Express.*
And 25 years' worth of interviews with many of the personalities mentioned in this book.